THE
MACMILLAN
BOOK
OF NATURAL HERB GARDENING

MARIE-LUISE KREUTER

THE MACMILLAN BOOK

OF NATURAL HERB GARDENING

Translated by Susan H. Ray

COLLIER BOOKS
MACMILLAN PUBLISHING COMPANY
New York

COLLIER MACMILLAN PUBLISHERS
London

Macmillan Publishing Company
866 Third Avenue, New York, N.Y. 10022
Collier Macmillan Canada, Inc.

Title of the original German edition:
DER NATURGEMÄSSE KRÄUTER-
GARTEN
© 1983 BLV Verlagsgesellschaft mbH,
München

English translation copyright © 1985 by
Macmillan Publishing Company,
a division of Macmillan, Inc.

**Library of Congress Cataloging in
Publication Data**
Kreuter, Marie-Luise.
    The Macmillan book of natural herb
gardening.

    Translation of: Der naturgemässe
Kräutergarten.
    Includes index
    1. Herb gardening. 2. Organic
gardening. 3. Herbs. I. Macmillan
Publishing Company. II. Title
SB351.H5K7413   1985   635'.7   85–7276
ISBN 0-02-063140-5

Macmillan books are available at special
discounts for bulk purchases for sales
promotions, premiums, fund-raising, or
educational use.

For details, contact:

Special Sales Director
Macmillan Publishing Company
866 Third Avenue
New York, N.Y. 10022

10 9 8 7 6 5 4 3 2 1

Printed in Germany

Contents

5

Introduction

Spice and medicinal herbs have led an "underground" life for most of the 20th century. The glories of progress were so blinding that thousand-year-old experiences were simply pushed aside as old-fashioned and superfluous. Pills replaced camomile in medicine chests, and the mugwort along the roadside was considered nothing more than a burdensome nuisance. People forgot that mugwort leaves make the Christmas goose easier to digest and that they can also alleviate stomachaches.

Fields as they used to be, with camomile and poppies.

As farmers cleared the edges of their fields with herbicides and fertilized their meadows with nitrogen-containing products, innumerable herbs also disappeared from daily view. Medicinal herbs were degraded to the status of weeds and, as an unwelcome evil along the road, cast aside in favor of ever more abundant harvests. Common primrose and salad burnet, camomile and field thyme fell into oblivion just as quickly as did field pansies, yarrow, wild peppermint, and corn poppies. Is there anyone who can still recognize these plants on sight? What child can still roam about and innocently pick bouquets of field flowers and learn to recognize and differentiate between the many varieties of fragrant "weeds"? Even their mothers are no longer certain; instead of brewing up a pot of natural fennel tea, they give their children presweetened commercial drinks that rot their teeth!

The variety of dishes in the kitchen has been reduced; the putting up or freezing of natural garden products is rapidly disappearing from households where working mothers find they have less and less time for such domestic chores. Parsley and chives from the supermarket usually make up the only fresh herbs in their kitchens—an unimaginative green monotony in comparison to the aromatic kitchens of our grandmothers. In those days marjoram, thyme, tarragon, and

Herbs that were known hundreds of years ago: thyme and hyssop with its blue blossoms.

borage still ranked as indispensable seasonings for tasty and easily digested meals. These kitchen herbs grew in the garden amid vegetables and flowers. They could always be picked fresh and thus tasted all the more delicious. Yet these plants gradually disappeared from the gardens, too; the unpretentious but fragrant herbs had to give way to magnificent roses and colorful summer flowers. Today's gardens emphasize the ornamental; they serve as oases for leisure activities and sometimes even to boost the gardener's sense of identity.

However, times are changing again. Belief in the never-ending progress of science and industry has been shaken. We are beginning to realize that technical conveniences must not be allowed to proceed at the cost of the environment. The desire for natural, healthy living conditions is gaining adherents everywhere you look. And this is where the good old herb plants reenter the picture. When suffering from the common cold, young women—just like their foremothers many years ago—are once again turning to linden-blossom teas and garden sage instead of antibiotics.

In the kitchen, too, young cooks are returning to rosemary, thyme, and sweet marjoram. Smells of Provençal herbs emanate from crock pots, and salad bowls smell of borage and dill. The desire to harvest all of these spicy ingredients fresh from one's own garden is only the logical result of this healthy as well as fragrant development.

This book will tell you how you

A spring snack with cress and radishes.

can raise the familiar as well as some of the more obscure kitchen herbs in your own garden. Their care is simple and uncomplicated once you know a little bit about the individual habits of these plants. Many medicinal plants that are being increasingly eliminated from open fields will find a new home in your garden. You will learn to recognize them by their leaves and blossoms once you start to live with them on a daily basis, and you will soon become thoroughly familiar with their good qualities.

These aromatic herbs with their valuable ingredients represent, especially for an organic garden, an enrichment that no good organic gardener can afford to renounce. Several of these medicinal and spice plants even play an important role in the control of garden pests; others serve as a source of nectar for bees and other useful insects. For all of these reasons, then, herbs contribute not only to the prosperity of the gardener and of his or her family as well but also to the healthy growth of other garden plants.

This book is primarily meant to give you, the reader, practical tips on how to set up your own herb garden. You will learn what has to be done to promote the healthy growth of your spice and medicinal plants. Natural methods of care and fertilization are very important aspects of this, for you will certainly want to harvest most of your herbs fresh from the garden and add them directly to your dishes. It would be quite absurd if you were to treat precisely these medicinal plants with poisonous concoctions.

You will also learn many ways to harvest and preserve your home-grown herbs. Recipes and "prescriptions," however, have been kept to a minimum—to just a taste, as it were. You can always increase your knowledge of spicy herb seasonings and old home remedies by referring to special literature on these topics. Here you will become personally acquainted with the herbs that are briefly described in the second half of the book. Only after you have visited "your" sage bush on a hot summer day in your own garden, after you have breathed in the intense and spicy fragrance of its silvery-green leaves, will you begin to appreciate just what riches are buried in these modest plants. Herbal friendships grow by themselves and last a lifetime.

A Remembrance of Days Gone By

The Troubled History of Herbs

Traces of green herbs reach back into dim antiquity. Wild-growing medicinal plants and spicy leaves, roots, or seeds that enrich the menu were already known to the people of the Stone Age. Like the Indians or the native tribes of the South Seas, these people lived on a very familiar basis with nature. Precise observation and the collected experience of many generations indicate that they had a reliable knowledge about the plants in their environment. Excavations of the stake huts of the early Stone Age have revealed seeds of the poppy, angelica, and caraway plants. But this is surely only a small selection of a much more varied spice "cabinet." After all, green leaves are ephemeral and leave no archeological traces behind!

More precise information concerning the history of herbs has come down to us via the written accounts of ancient civilizations.

Thousands of years before Christ, the Chinese and the Sumerians consolidated their knowledge or herbs and wrote it down for posterity. In India, Egypt, and Babylonia, medicinal plants were similarly collected and cultivated. We still come across several of them in our own gardens and kitchens today: thyme, caraway, bay leaves, dill, and fennel.

Even the foundations of our Central European herb gardens

The historic herb garden at Marksburg on the Rhine.

A Remembrance of Days Gone By

were laid in Greek and Roman antiquity. Famous physicians and botanists of those times studied the medicinal plants indigenous to their countries. They later were responsible for world-famous writings based upon their own observations and experiences.

At the dawn of modern times, Hippocrates, Theophrastus, Galen, and Dioscorides had a great influence on the medicinal and healing powers of plants in the Western World. Knowledge of herbs from ancient Rome was left to us by Pliny the Elder and Columella. The actual cultivation of an herb garden, however, goes back to the Benedictine monks who wandered across the Alps in order to convert the Franks and the Germanic tribes to Christianity. In addition to the Bible, their luggage contained the seeds of important medicinal and spice plants that were indigenous to the lands surrounding the Mediterranean Sea. This is how sage, garlic, thyme, rosemary, common rue, and many another important herb found their way into medieval cloister gardens.

Charlemagne, too, did his part in spreading the spice plants that have since enriched our kitchens and home medicine chests. In his famous *Capitulare de villis,* an ordinance for imperial landholdings, he described in great detail in 812 just exactly which herbs should be planted in his gardens.

A splendid list was thus put together which included, among others, sage, muscatel sage, common rue, southernwood, rosemary, caraway, anise, cress, parsley, celery, lovage, dill, fennel, mustard, summer savory, curly mint, wild mint, chives, onions, garlic, coriander, and chervil. One of today's herb gardens would be hard put to offer such an abundance as this.

In the course of centuries, these herbs slowly wandered beyond the walls protecting the cloister and palace gardens and into the gardens of peasants. And when the art of printing was invented toward the end of the Middle Ages, it provided the vehicle for transmitting the knowledge of these medicinal plants together with many recipes to "the common folk." In the books of the well-known herbalists like Otto Brunfels, Leonhard Fuchs, Hieronymus Bosch, Petrus Andreas Matthiolus, and Johann Teodor Tabernaemontanus, anyone who was literate could "read up" on the mysterious properties of these herbs and how they worked. Knowledge from antiquity and the Middle Ages was collected in these comprehensive books, written clearly in the German language. Even today these works continue to represent a solid source of information for anyone who takes the trouble to work his or her way through the thick folios. Moreover, they are once again available, this time in facsimile editions in bookshops specializing in such works.

The printed as well as the spoken word formed an unbroken

A flourishing spice and medicinal-plant garden near an old Swedish house in Ystad.

chain of transmission of knowledge about these medicinal plants up to the beginning of the 20th century. It also sometimes happened that ancient stories and magical rites concerning popular "holy herbs" gained adherents. Nevertheless, people have maintained their familiarity with these extraordinary plants in their daily lives. Their use in many areas of life far outweighed their occasional misuse. It took the onset of the age of industry and technology to disrupt the transmission of these experiences and personal knowledge handed down from one generation to another. And many recipes were thus lost and forgotten.

A Remembrance of Days Gone By

Ancient Herbs Rediscovered

For about 50 years—from somewhere in the 1920's to the 1970's—we believed that we could do without something as "primitive" as the simple herbs along the roadside. Medical science was conquered by the rapidly working pills and injections of chemical therapy. The important remedies no longer came from nature, but rather from a test tube in a factory somewhere.

Many natural products, among them the diverse variety of herbs, also disappeared from the kitchen. Instead of using the juice of red beets, cooks began to color their food with artificial ingredients; genuine vanilla beans were replaced by handy but synthetically produced vanilla sugars. The art of cooking became more and more impoverished while preserves and frozen meals supposedly simplified life. Homemade dishes were relegated to the kitchens of "country folk." Modern people no longer considered it necessary to spend their energy

A motley farmer's garden with herbs (foreground), vegetables, and medicinal pot marigolds.

A Remembrance of Days Gone By

on growing their own cabbage. Most of them did not even notice that the transition of their kitchen gardens into ornamental oases cost them the harvest of these modest herbs.

The realization that progress brought in its wake dangerous losses to the quality of life first became widespread in the seventies. Many people were once again concerned about the fact that nature cannot simply be neglected with impunity. In the meantime, however, millions of us had become accustomed to an excessive consumption of pills and had to pay for this with frequently unpleasant side effects. Every day more and more harmful ingredients are being discovered in commercially available foodstuffs. Recollections and reminiscences about the simpler and healthier way of life began to take hold. In this anxiety-causing situation, in which the monster Progress has already cast dark shadows over all areas of one's private life, many people have also rediscovered the advantages of simple herbs.

Medicinal plants are just as reliable today as they were thousands of years ago in their role as an effective remedy for many common ailments. They have no dangerous side effects. Of course, no one should take these natural medicaments frivolously. A visit to the doctor is absolutely essential with serious disorders. And remember: Before you use medicinal herbs, make sure you know exactly what you are taking.

Herb seedlings like these can be purchased.

But how can we, today, ask our grandmothers for their camomile recipes? Obviously, books and lectures will have to fill in the gaps between the generations and transmit anew the knowledge of these medicinal herbs "among the people."

There is an advantage here, though, because the newest scientific insights can be passed on as well as the old experiences. Many ingredients in the most popular herbs can be isolated and studied in great detail by means of chemical analysis. In this way the positive effects of herbs that have been known for so long can be retroactively identified and confirmed.

Various herbal teas from your own garden make valuable natural remedies.

There is also a renewed need for spices and herbs in the kitchen. Many people have become acquainted with the taste of various herbs during their vacation trips and return from Italy or Spain with the recipe for an aromatic rosemary chicken dish or for a tomato salad with basil. The demand for a larger selection of fresh herbs has thus increased considerably. Even the supermarkets are now offering spicy delicacies such as tarragon, lemon balm, and lovage. The best and most intensive aromas, however, still come from herbs that you harvest absolutely fresh from your own garden or windowsill and add directly to your food. And not only gourmets profit from this, for each spice plant is at the same time a medicinal herb. An imaginative herb cook thus con-stantly provides her family with natural green medicaments. Sweet marjoram on a roast repre-sents a kindness to your stomach and your digestive system; lemon balm in the salad has a slightly soothing effect on agitated nerves.

It goes without saying that many organic gardeners, who very consciously plant medicinal herbs in their vegetable beds, have contributed a great deal to the rediscovery of herbs. In so doing, they frequently refer back to the experiences of old peasant farmers. I hope that this book will tempt and encourage you, too, to plant as many herbs as possible in your own garden. You will do much more than simply redis-cover the enchanting fragrance of days gone by; herbs can provide healthy joys in many aspects of your life.

A Place for Fresh Herbs

Every garden has some space left over for a small selection of herbs, but just make sure it is not an accidental corner, for these spicy plants need good living conditions in order to develop their valuable ingredients. If they are planted in proper locations, their care will present no problem, for herbs thrive just as well on the edge of a vegetable garden as they do in a box in the kitchen window.

Forest mallows grow on sunny roadsides.

The Ideal Location

The majority of herb plants as well as many medicinal plants are indigenous to the warm lands surrounding the Mediterranean Sea. Although they became accustomed to more rugged climates thousands of years ago, they are still not able to renounce two things: light and warmth. Always choose the sunniest spot in your garden or near the house for your herbs. The location should be as protected as possible. The plants find that a spot in front of a bright southern wall, for example, provides ideal "native" conditions.

Light humus soil with good drainage provides the best foundation for these Mediterranean plants that frequently flourish on dry cliffsides or in steppelike regions in their native habitat. Too much nourishment and too much water harm most herbs. Among the southerners that prefer sunny but otherwise rather ascetic living conditions are rosemary, lavender, thyme, sweet marjoram, common rue, sage, hyssop, southernwood, summer savory, wild marjoram, lemon balm, coriander, and fennel.

Other plants that are indigenous to Central Europe also thrive in our herb gardens. Several still grow in their wild form in meadows, along the banks of streams, or along the sides of roads. Some of them prefer somewhat moister, more nutritious conditions than those to which they are accustomed in their natural habitats.

Wild lavender grows on warm cliffs.

A Place for Fresh Herbs

A large herb bed with borage (foreground), tarragon (right), and lemon balm.

They can also tolerate some shade. Some of the herbs that stem from indigenous wild plants include garden sorrel, scurvy grass, winter cress, mugwort, common wormwood, angelica, salad burnet, peppermint, chives, caraway, and celery.

Unsuitable for all herbs are locations in deep shade, as, for example, beneath trees. Drafty corners should also be avoided, as well as poor ventilation due to overcrowded conditions. Herbs cannot tolerate heavy soils or standing water at all. You should either avoid locations such as these completely or improve them considerably by adding drainage and loosening the soil. You will always reap the best results if you treat your herbs the way nature intended.

The Arrangement of an Herb Garden

There is no ideal size or shape to an herb garden. It should be flexible enough to fit in completely with the size of the plot and the desires of the gardener. Of course, it would be ideal if you could arrange an isolated herb garden within the parameters of your vegetable, fruit, or ornamental garden. Divide this area up into several small beds and leave space for narrow paths between them. Low box-tree hedges can

A Place for Fresh Herbs

serve as a green boundary screening off the herb region from the rest of the garden. The herb gardens in old cloisters or palace parks were arranged in a similar fashion—strict and clear.

The subdivisions into individual beds provide an attractive picture of old-fashioned charm, but they are also practical at the same time. You can keep an overview of the various herbs and care for them easily in keeping with their different habits and needs. The paths make planting, sowing, weeding, and watering that much easier, and each plant will be within easy reach when it comes time to harvest your crop.

Roof tiles, flagstones, cement blocks, and plaster tiles are all suitable materials for the walks or narrow paths. Wooden beams or railroad ties blend in very well with the image of a natural herb garden. Gravel paths are reminiscent of old farmers' gardens. They set a certain mood and tone, but they also require a good deal of work, because they frequently have to be raked smooth.

Neither the paths nor the beds of an herb garden need be absolutely straight. Gently winding paths and rounded or ornamental beds can have a very attractive

The beds in this historic herb garden are enclosed by boxwood hedges.

A Place for Fresh Herbs

Herbs along the edges of vegetable beds.

Herbs among summer flowers and vegetable plants.

effect. The actual shape and arrangement is totally dependent upon the temperament and taste of the individual gardener. The illustrations in this chapter are meant to serve merely as suggestions that might tantalize your own imagination.

Fragrant Borders and Hedges

If you do not have enough room for an enclosed herb garden, you can reserve a narrow strip for spice plants along the edge of your vegetable garden. Even a bed 3' by 10' or 16' offers enough room for an interesting selection. Here you can plant a colorful mixture of fragrant spice plants which provide an attractive and decorative sight. A border of plants that are as useful as they are pretty thus outlines one side of the vegetable garden.

The "skeleton" of this planting should consist of durable shrub herbs that can be allowed to spread out over a long period of time in the same location. The following plants are suitable for this purpose: sage, lavender, southernwood, hyssop, wild marjoram, thyme, wild thyme, common rue, wormwood, lemon balm, and costmary. The intensely fragrant sage plant develops into a knee-high, woody shrub with narrow greenish-gray leaves and bluish-violet blossoms. There are, in addition, very attractive multicolored-leaved varieties that all stem from the spice and medicinal sage plant *(Salvia officinalis)*. A small concentration of these shrubs has a very picturesque effect. Ornamental sage with its iridescent, candle-shaped blossoms, on the other hand, has no "edible" value for an herb or spice border. The best you can do is add it as a distant relative and

A Place for Fresh Herbs

colorful focus of attention wherever you need or want a more dramatic statement.

Lavender, hyssop, and wild marjoram also introduce color and attractive blossoms to your borders. Common rue, southernwood, and mugwort contribute to the beauty of your arrangement with their particularly decorative leaves. The edge of the bed can be enclosed with low bolsters of thyme or wild thyme. Sufficient space usually remains free between these perennial shrubs to sow a small selection of annual herbs. These may include sweet marjoram, summer savory, basil, and chervil, all according to your taste. This type of border is enhanced by the strong, very different aromas that emanate from the individual plants. The actual choice is determined solely by the combination of scents.

Several shrublike herbs can also be used to form hedges. They can tolerate being cut back with garden shears and are thus very appropriate for thick, low enclosures similar to the box-tree hedges in a farmer's garden. You can use them to line beds or paths, and your every step through your summer garden will be accompanied by glorious fragrances—not to mention the additional advantage of being able to harvest spice leaves for the kitchen or the teapot.

The following plants make good, low, fragrant hedges: lavender, southernwood, lavender cotton, and low varieties of com-

A trimmed lavender hedge in bloom.

Variegated sage (*Salvia* "Tricolor").

mon wormwood. More detailed descriptions of lavender, southernwood, and wormwood can be found in the second half of this book. Lavender cotton is not an edible plant, but it does represent a pleasant-smelling supplement to your herb garden. Its fragrant silvery-gray leaves blend in well with the other spice plants, which

A Place for Fresh Herbs

are predominantly green, gray, or silver.

Companions for Summer Flowers

Many spice and tea herbs are strikingly decorative. Their frequently ornamental leaves and colorful blossoms turn them into small jewels that would grace any ornamental garden. It follows, then, that if you have even a small garden with just a few bushes, roses, and summer flowers behind your house, you need not renounce these herbs. Simply smuggle them in between the ornamentals. In this way the pleasant can be combined with the practical.

For example, in the foreground of your shrub bed you can plant sage, lavender, wild marjoram, common rue, hyssop, and costmary between the daisies, bluebells, and milfoil. Among the medium and tall shrubs in the background you can introduce elecampane, tea fennel, angelica, and lovage. Thyme or stonecrop forms pleasant bolsters along the edge of the bed. Even chive bushes give the appearance of cheerful bouquets during their blooming season. A bunch of deep green parsley or a corner of blooming summer savory can be skillfully combined with some of your summer shrubs.

Annual and biennial summer flowers also make good companions for herbs without appearing too foreign. Here the line dividing

the practical and the ornamental is very fluid. Pot marigolds, common nasturtiums, mullein, and mallows belong among the familiar summer beauties of the flower garden just as much as they do to the ancient medicinal plants.

Several borage plants can also have a very pretty effect in an ornamental garden. Their star-shaped blossoms in sky blue and pink attract bees and insects in droves. This robust herb, however, does need a generous amount of space and can easily overpower the more delicate flowers in its vicinity.

Purslane, the delicately pinnate coriander, scurvy grass, and winter purslane can likewise be mixed in among your summer flowers as well as a little sweet marjoram, cress, and chervil.

In the colorful rural gardens of the turn of the century there was no strict division between the

Blooming neighbors: daisies and dill.

Circular beds with chives, summer flowers, and vegetables.

Lavender and thyme in a mixed planting with shrubs and woody plants.

kitchen and the ornamental gardens. A cheerful confusion reigned among the herbs, flowers, and lettuces. Kitchen and medicinal plants were usually combined with shrubs and summer flowers to form a colorful border surrounding the vegetable beds. Next to sage, summer savory, wormwood, fennel, lemon balm, parsley, dill, and borage used to grow the charming flowers that have been at home in rural gardens for hundreds of years: marigolds, Madonna lilies, wallflowers, irises, peonies, columbine, daisies, bleeding hearts, violets, and oxeye daisies. You, too, can choose this pleasant mixture from the old days as a model for your small but colorful herb garden.

A Place for Fresh Herbs

Finally, a whole series of spice plants can also thrive in a rock garden. It is primarily the herbs from the Mediterranean regions that love this type of location. Of course, the mountain plants of a rock garden need just as much sun, as poor a soil, and as good drainage as these herbs do. Thus you can plant lavender, thyme, wild thyme, hyssop, sage, southernwood, common rue, wild marjoram, Roman camomile, mint, and stonecrop in rock gardens. In such a sunny location, even rosemary feels at home during the summer if you bury it in its pot. Just remember that this herb is not winter-hardy.

A Small Kitchen Garden

Housewives and people who like to cook find it practical to have fresh herbs at their fingertips when they work in the kitchen. This is the obvious solution if your property is small. You can start a mobile herb garden in pots, tubs, and boxes in front of a warm, protected southern exposure of the house or perhaps directly on the terrace. A sunny southwestern corner is also suitable for this purpose. An eastern exposure is too cold in the winter and does not receive enough sun; the shady, cold northern exposure is totally unsuited for herbs. The larger the receptacles are, the better the living conditions they can offer the plants. The roots can spread out, and water and nutrients are not used up as

quickly. Very tall pots or tubs are needed only for plants with very deep root systems. As a general rule, broad dishes, medium-sized clay flower pots, and broad window boxes are sufficient.

If you want your small kitchen garden to be pretty as well as practical, you might opt to use decorative terra-cotta planters, rustic stoneware jugs, and wooden boxes. The components of such a mobile herbal community are obviously very variable. They will always reflect the taste of the individual gardener and can be varied from year to year.

Most of the annual and biennial herbs can be sown in boxes and bowls. You should keep the perennial shrubs in their own pots or boxes because they will need special care during the winter. Rosemary, for example, is not winter-hardy. This small shrub must be brought indoors in the fall. It can spend the winter with no danger whatsoever in a cool but bright spot. Under these conditions you can keep potted sage, thyme, hyssop, and southernwood in the house during the cold season. Even so, these plants may be left outside. Since smaller containers freeze through quickly, you will have to protect them against the cold. Ideal for this purpose would be a large carton with moist peat in which you then bury the pots. A plastic sheet can also serve as a protective covering in emergency situations.

On the other hand, boxes and flower pots dry out rapidly on hot spring and summer days. You will

A Place for Fresh Herbs

have to water them generously—the best times to do this are in the morning and again every evening. Add an organic fertilizer such as horn shavings as a time-release source of nutrients. This can be mixed into the soil in the spring.

You might also want to put little laurel trees, rosemary bushes, and myrtle in decorative tub planters in your kitchen garden. Even roses can live for a certain length of time in large planters of this kind. Simple varieties of dog roses blend in best with herbs and medicinal plants. Besides their beauty and their enchanting fragrances, they also contribute medicinal ingredients. Advanced herb gardeners toss fresh rose petals into their bath and use them as seasoning in old-fashioned desserts and beverages.

An abundant variety of kitchen spices in a sizable wooden planter.

Growing Spices on the Balcony or Terrace

Even if you have only a balcony, you can comfortably join the ranks of herb gardeners. As was already mentioned in the section on the kitchen garden, many spice plants readily adapt to life in a box. You have your choice among cress, chervil, dill, borage, purslane, sweet marjoram, basil, summer savory, and parsley.

The following shrub herbs also feel at home for a period of time in boxes or larger tubs: sage, thyme, tarragon, wild marjoram, hyssop, lemon balm, and peppermint. However, they seldom last as long as they would in the garden. Still, in the meantime you can propagate these plants by taking and planting your own cuttings.

When preparing your boxes and pots or tubs, be sure you always make appropriate drainage systems. Every container must have large holes in its base. Place a few pieces of broken clay flower pots or flat flintstones over these openings so that they do not clog up. Then fill in the lowest layer with about ½" to ¾" of sand or gravel.

In most instances, commercially available potting soil is not good for spice plants. These soils

Spring flowers and herbs make an attractive combination (above). Spice plants are within handy reach in front of the window (middle). Decorative laurel tree (below).

A Place for Fresh Herbs

consist primarily of peat and are thus very sour. If it is at all possible, you should mix the soil for your balcony or window boxes yourself out of equal amounts of ripe compost, sand, and peat. Just before planting you might want to toss into the partially filled boxes horn shavings as a source of nutrients. Two handfuls of fertilizer are sufficient for a box 3′ long. Mix the horn shavings in with the humus and then fill in the rest of the soil. This supply will feed the herbs for one entire summer. Only when the boxes are very densely overgrown or when they are mixed with summer flowers should you add a little liquid manure to the root area sometime between June and August. Guano diluted in the watering can is good for this purpose, as are other organic liquid manures and liquid fertilizers.

Herb boxes on the balcony are particularly charming if they are interspersed with flowers. Of course, the combination of herb plants and summer flowers must make sense together. In this regard, common nasturtiums blend in well in such a community, because their iridescent yellow or orange blossoms are as attractive as they are appetizing. Heliotrope, marigolds, sweet-smelling alyssum, summer carnations, and the old, fragrant mignonette also form harmonious complements to spicy herb plants.

Growing Herbs on the Windowsill

The smallest fragrance-and-spice garden can take shape on a bright, warm windowsill. A modest selection of herbs is easily accommodated there in flower pots and bowls. Once in a while a few leaves can be picked for use in the kitchen, but these plants should never be plundered because they will then lose their attractive appearance.

Peppery basil plants frequently flourish better in flower pots on a warm windowsill than in the open garden. Even rosemary lends itself well to cultivation on a windowsill. Thyme, sage, hyssop, and lemon balm also thrive in a flower pot if given proper attention. Chives, parsley, and "happy-go-lucky" cress are naturals for the windowsill nursery.

The ingredients for a homemade soil mixture for a window box.

Planning an Herb Garden

Herbs thrive in balcony boxes, too.

If you are fond of a nostalgic atmosphere, you might want to plant a collection of enchanting, scented-leaved geraniums. Depending upon the variety, these plants give off the scents of lemons, roses, peppermint, or apples. Unfortunately, these old-fashioned treasures are seldom for sale, but new plants grow easily from cuttings. They thus travel from hand to hand and house to house.

Preparing the Soil

Once you have chosen an appropriate spot in the garden for your herbs, the preparation of the soil is one of the most important tasks awaiting you. You know, of course, that loose soil and a good drainage system are the basics that ensure healthy growth. Examine your garden soil to determine its type:

- Friable, slightly sandy humus is ideal.
- Heavy, dense, loamy soil has to be loosened at all costs. You can use pure sand and a regular dose of compost to accomplish this. A deep-rooting green manure is also a very effective method, but it should be sown over the whole surface one year prior to the planting of the herb garden.
- Poor, sandy soil is good for the spice plants from the south. You might want to improve it a bit by adding powdered clay and compost. With the passage of time this will make the soil more cohesive and richer in humus.

From left to right: chives, thyme, lemon balm, borage, basil, rosemary.

Planning an Herb Garden

If your garden has a very heavy clay soil that collects water in its underlying layers, you have no choice but to build in a drainage layer. Given these unfavorable conditions, it would be best to erect an elevated bed for your herbs.

The first step is to dig a hole about 12″ to 20″ deep in the entire surface of the intended bed. The bottom layer of this ditch should then be filled with coarse gravel, followed by a layer of sand. On top of this you should pile cut-up tree debris or underbrush. Only then can you add humus. Loosen this garden soil thoroughly before planting, too; the best method is to mix in generous amounts of compost, sand, and some peat.

Enclose this bed with a border about 12″ to 20″ high made of railroad ties or treated logs. Also suitable are quarry stones that can be piled up to make a dry wall. In this way you can elevate your herb bed above the heavy soil of the garden and at the same time provide good drainage.

Compost Is Indispensable

The best way to care for the soil in your herb garden is to give it regular doses of compost. This homemade supersoil that emerges from the debris of the gardening year forms the foundation of every natural-care program. Even if you have only a small plot, there will always be enough space to set up a compost silo in the shade of a bush or shrub. If you have more room at your disposal, you can erect a proper compost area with heaps, silos, and liquid-manure barrels.

The basic recipe for compost is the same for any arrangement. Collect the organic waste of the garden, such as wilted flowers, cabbage leaves, bean stalks, hedge clippings, and grass. Even kitchen waste, such as potato peels, leftover vegetables, coffee grounds, tea, and cut flowers, can be used.

The first step is to chop up these various materials into, at the most, hand-sized pieces, using either a spade or a pair of garden shears. A shredder or grinder can take care of this task particularly quickly and efficiently. The smaller the pieces of waste when they arrive at the compost heap, the quicker they will decompose into precious humus.

Another important point: Be sure you always mix the dry and the wet substances together very thoroughly, for the compost heap should be neither putrefyingly wet nor hard and dry. Always pile up a fairly large amount in the silo or on the heap, because flat surfaces do not heat up sufficiently. In the first phase of decomposition, your compost has to generate a certain amount of heat so that the rotting process can proceed uninterruptedly.

Always pile up layers about 8″ high and then sprinkle a little organic fertilizer and pulverized (preferably algal) limestone on

A compost silo needs very little space.

Fertilizing with compost in the spring.

top. You may also want to add a compost starter (various organic products are commercially available). These preparations accelerate the decomposition process.

You can get the same favorable effect if you distribute a few shovelfuls of compost from an already constructed heap in among the waste materials. This soil is crawling with useful fungi and ground bacteria that play an important role in decomposition. They act like a positive injection and set the breakdown process in motion.

As a protection against cold, dampness, and wind, finished compost heaps can be covered over with a coat of straw, leaves, grass, or even old sacks. You should place a plastic sheet over a silo only when beset with continuously rainy weather. A warm leaf cover can be spread on top of the compost heap as an uppermost layer during the winter. For a successful production of compost, make sure you abide by these important rules:

- Compost needs light and oxygen; this is why the material has to be loose at all times.
- Compost needs warmth; this is why you have to pile it at least 20″ high and cover it over. Once this is done, the decomposition process will generate sufficient heat.
- Compost needs moisture; this is why you have to make sure you have a "juicy mixture" and why you must water the heap in dry weather.

Depending upon its composition, the compost heap should be

ripe and ready to use in about 7 to 12 months. By this time all waste materials have been transformed into fragrant, nutrient-containing humus. For your herb garden, you should always use ripe compost that has completely turned to soil. Coarse compost is not recommended here.

Spread the compost over the whole surface of the bed about ¾" to 1" deep and lightly rake it into the ground. It is a good idea to put an additional dose around the herb shrubs in spring or fall.

In organic gardens this compost should be covered with grass, leaves, or some other organic waste so that it remains moist. Since numerous herbs, however, not only tolerate but also prefer dryness, you should not use a soft mulch layer for this purpose. Cover with flat stones those places that are not in the shade of your herb plants. Stones containing lime are particularly conducive to the growth of sage, hyssop, and southernwood. And there is yet another advantage here, since stones keep the warmth in.

Herbs Should Not Be Overfed

Most herbs actually prefer a rather poor soil. If they are given too much nourishment, they shoot up into luxuriant plants but develop few aromatic and medicinal properties. Strong or rapidly dissipating nitrogen-containing fertilizers should therefore be avoided by all means in an herb garden. Gourmet diets were not meant for herbs or spice plants. A slight fast, on the other hand, has a very favorable effect.

As a rule, a regular application of compost provides a sufficient amount of nutrient reserves. Nevertheless, if you occasionally want to add a little extra nourishment to very poor soils or to very vigorously growing plants (see the section entitled "The Ideal Location" p. 15), you would do best to choose an organic fertilizer that is only very slowly released into the soil. Examples of this are horn shavings or a mixture of horn-blood-and-bone meal that you can spread around the plants in early spring; rake it in slightly and cover it with compost. A dose of very diluted stinging-nettle liquid manure is also allowed in early summer. But never forget: Too little is better than too much.

Sowing Annual and Biennial Herbs

Loosen the beds once again with a trowel or a garden "fork" prior to planting. Carefully remove all weeds with their roots intact. Collect all stones and coarse clumps of earth and carry them away. The soil should be delicate, friable, and loose. After the herb beds have been treated with compost, rake the surface smooth and divide up the area for the individual plants. Be generous here, so that the plants will have enough

Planning an Herb Garden

room and light later on to ensure a healthy growth.

Using a stick or even your finger, draw flat gooves for the various seeds. Always put the seed package or a name plate next to the area you have just planted so that you will be able to identify the seedlings as they appear. This small precautionary measure is particularly important for beginners; after a few years of observation you will be able to differentiate the herbs without such assistance as soon as the

The liquid manure made from stinging nettles must be greatly diluted.

first green leaves poke through the ground.

Never start to sow too early. The soil must have had enough time to warm up so that the seeds will germinate. Also, never work in wet, sticky earth. If the humus falls apart by itself into loose, moist crumbs, it is ready to offer the new seeds the prerequisites for a "soft bed."

In mild climates you can sow insensitive herbs like parsley, cress, and chervil as early as March. Follow these in April with borage, dill, caraway, scurvy grass, and pot marigolds. You will have to wait for warm May days before you can plant sweet marjoram, summer savory, basil, purslane, nasturtiums, and celery in your open garden. Biennial herbs like parsley and scurvy grass can be reseeded in late summer.

The best time to sow and the recommended distances between the rows are indicated on the seed packages. You will also find this information included in the descriptions of the herbs later in the book. Fill the seed grooves with finely sifted compost and distribute the seeds as sparingly and as evenly as possible, within the stipulations on the seed package. As a last step you should cover the rows with a thin layer of soil and water them carefully. This area has to be kept uniformly moist until the seeds germinate. One suggestion you might try is to place damp sacks over the beds on hot spring days. Several herbs, such as summer savory

Planning an Herb Garden

Carefully prepared herb seedbed.

and cress, for example, tend to grow without crowding. All you have to do is thin them out a bit later on. Others have to be separated as soon as the plants are

large enough to allow this. These plants include basil, common nasturtiums, and sweet marjoram. You will find all further details in the descriptions of the individual herbs.

Early Cultivation of Sensitive Herbs

Several particularly warmth-loving spice plants wilt easily in an open garden when spring turns cool. Sow these children of the south preferably under a protective roof. Basil and marjoram will be grateful for such attention. You can begin sowing these plants in an enclosed hotbed or under a plastic sheet in early April. Less sensitive herbs germinate there as early as March.

The soil in these arrangements should be prepared in the same way as for the open garden and it should be watered regularly. The seeds germinate very rapidly in

After only 10 days, cress seeds produce vigorous green leaves.

Planning an Herb Garden

the humid atmosphere under glass or plastic. You must remember to ventilate them during the day when the weather is warm to avoid the buildup of any condensation.

Herbs find especially conducive growing conditions in small greenhouses in spring. If the house is heated, you can begin to sow there as early as January.

But there are other, less work-intensive approaches: Put a small window greenhouse or a few flower pots on a bright, warm windowsill. Place shards over the drainage holes in the bottom of these receptacles and fill them with an initial layer of sand followed by a layer of loose soil mixed well with sand. Now you can distribute the seeds sparingly and cover them over with finely sifted compost. Use your fingers to press the soil firmly in place and moisten it very carefully with lukewarm water.

The small, indoor hothouse or greenhouse should then be covered with a transparent cover. Place a pane of glass over the flower pots. A plastic bag, such as are used to store food in the refrigerator, can be fastened with a rubber band and makes a very serviceable cover. As soon as the green plants pop up, you must ventilate the pots on the windowsill. A lot of light and fresh air will ensure that the small herbs do not turn into tall and lanky weaklings. Draughts, however, should be avoided.

As soon as you can grasp the little plants between your fingers, you should transplant them individually or in small groups in clay flower pots or peat containers. Here they will develop strong and vigorous roots. Starting about the middle of May, when the last danger of frost is past, you can plant these herbs in the open garden. The location should be a warm and sunny one.

Transplanting Perennial Herbs

You can plant perennial herb shrubs in the open garden either in the spring or in the fall. They are usually purchased in pots and are thus well rooted and promise good growth. Naturally, you may also use this time to relocate the durable spice plants that you have either raised from seed or propagated by means of cuttings.

The soil preparations are the same as those prescribed for sowing annual herbs. It is especially important to weed the shrub bed thoroughly before planting. This will spare you a lot of grief later on: in the course of time, spice plants grow together with couch grass, goutweed, or cocksfoot to form an impenetrable thicket of roots.

Choose with care the location for the shrubs and small, woody plants among your herbs. And while choosing, consider the size and the height of the mature plants so that you can allow for proper spacing between individuals. Herbs that grow too close together are susceptible to dis-

Herb seedlings in flower pots, peat pots, under a plastic hood, and in a "green-house."

Basil should be planted in bunches.

Individual plants grow vigorously.

Planning an Herb Garden

eases and insect pests. Remember how the bright southern light envelops these plants in their natural habitat. They should be provided with similar conditions in the garden.

Using a small shovel, dig a hole and fill it with ripe compost. Then position the root ball in the small hole and fill all around it with humus. Use your hands to press the earth down firmly so that it totally and tightly encompasses the roots. The plants should not be planted any deeper in the garden than they were in the pot. Water them very carefully, and if you take the trouble to make sure

You can buy small containers of herb shrubs in seedling form.

The bed for perennial herbs must be carefully prepared.

that the roots of the young plants never have a chance to dry out during the next few weeks, your shrub herbs will very quickly acclimatize themselves to their new environment. The first new shoots in the spring will indicate how well the shrubs have taken hold.

Propagating Your Own Herbs

You can propagate almost all of the perennial herbs yourself. It pays to sow from seed in a larger garden, for this ensures an abundance of small plants. You are best advised to use flat bowls that can be placed in a greenhouse or on a windowsill. These seedlings should be treated in keeping with the directions in the section entitled "Early Cultivation of Sensitive Herbs," p. 31. You can easily cultivate rosemary, sage, lavender, Russian tarragon, hyssop, lovage, and chives from seeds.

If you need only a few plants for the expansion or the rejuvenation of your herb garden, you should take some cuttings in the summer. Young, not yet woody twigs make the best cuttings. They should be removed with a sharp knife and put in small pots filled with a very sandy soil mixture. Remove all the leaves except the very top ones. Cuttings need uniform moisture; if they are too wet, the stems will rot.

Warmth and partial shade encourage the formation of roots. A greenhouse, a hotbed, or a pro-

tected garden spot makes the best nursery. As soon as the cuttings have developed strong roots and begin to set their own shoots, they should be transplanted into somewhat larger pots. You can try to propagate the following herbs with this method: sage, southernwood, winter savory, hyssop, wild marjoram, wormwood, lavender, tarragon, lemon balm, rosemary, and thyme.

Many plants naturally tend to produce sinker shoots. An old sage bush, for example, bends its branches toward the ground. When these are fastened down in the middle with a stone or some packed earth, the sage plant immediately sinks new roots. Later on you can cut the branch loose on the right and left and plant the new, rooted piece in a bed.

Propagation is particularly easy when the herb forms root runners. If this is the case, all you have to do is carefully dig up a piece of the root with some above-ground portions of the plant still attached and plant it somewhere else. The best time for this type of propagation is in the fall (October to November) and in the spring (April to May). Tarragon and peppermint are especially responsive to this method.

Finally, there are other perennial herbs that form a large, closed root system with many above-ground runners over a fairly long period of time. Like most shrubs, these plants can be dug up and divided into several

pieces. Pierce the root ball with a sharp spade and separate the densely grown confusion with several cuts from all sides. Follow this up by planting the newly formed bushes, but remember: Do not bury them any deeper than they originally were. In this way you can rejuvenate old spice shrubs and at the same time increase the number of your plants. Lemon balm, wild marjoram, and chives are all amenable to this form of propagation.

Finally, you can also multiply your lovage, horseradish, comfrey, elecampane, and garden sorrel by digging up individual roots or pieces of same. Always remember, though, that every division means a painful incision into the plant's life. Careful attention and a recuperation period are necessary to ensure that new life will develop. At such times, damp weather and cloudy skies are more helpful than burning sunshine.

Herb "Sources"

Seeds for many annual, biennial, and perennial herbs have recently become available all over in well-stocked nurseries and mail-order establishments. In addition to a wide selection, specialized firms also offer rarities for sale.

From top to bottom: Root runners of the tarragon plant; dividing root balls of lemon balm; sage seedlings.

Planning an Herb Garden

Young plants are usually available in local nurseries, in markets, and in garden centers. The consumer is free to choose his or her own plants as well as to examine the plants as to their quality. Since interest in herbs has grown so greatly in recent years, even gardeners are beginning to pay more attention to them. 10 years ago a poor herb gardener received an astonished shake of the head in response to his or her request for tarragon or sage; that same gardener today can choose among a large assortment of spice plants. This is a very gratifying development. If, in spite of all this, you still find it difficult to locate a source for fresh plants in your neighborhood, you can always resort to placing an order with a reputable shrub nursery or mail-order nursery. The herbs will come in the mail, having been cultivated in pots and firmly packed for shipping. By the way, a brief detour to a friendly neighbor also frequently results in many a rich source. If you have the opportunity, make the most of it and trade your herbs!

Fundamentals for Vigorous Growth

You lay the foundation for healthy growth in the truest sense of the word when you prepare and care for the soil in keeping with organic methods (see p. 26). Beyond that, however, it is also important to accept the natural conditions of climate and location. In very rugged regions with long, cold winters, you will have a hard time raising some tropical herbs. Some types of thyme, for example, will suffer from frost in such an environment. It is better to decide right from the start to cultivate more robust varieties of thyme.

All your herbs should be chosen with an eye to the climate to which they will be exposed. In a warm, grape-growing region an herb gardener can even afford to let his rosemary bush spend the winter in a protected corner of the garden. In higher altitudes this experiment would surely result in a great disappointment and a frozen plant. Read the descriptions of the individual plants in the second part of this book very carefully, and then decide which herbs will find the appropriate living conditions in your garden.

In an herb bed, just as in an organic vegetable garden, a rotating mixed-planting system produces favorable results. Each year you should sow the annual herbs in a different place, so that the soil does not become exhausted in a particular spot or way. You will see the success of this approach especially clearly in the case of parsley: this herb is incompatible with itself. It wilts away if it remains in the same place for any length of time.

Finally, you will be helping your spice plants on toward healthy growth if you make sure they are far enough apart from one another and have sufficient light. Borage, for example, is easily

The Organic Method of . . .

attacked by lice if the plants are very close together. On the other hand, if this robust herb were free to develop on all sides, the strong, hairy leaves would remain healthy. Since the black seeds are large enough to be grasped individually, you can make sure they have enough room when you plant them. Borage plants propagated in the wild have to be thinned out very early. These rules apply for most spice and medicinal plants. It is better to forgo an overabundant number so that your existing herbs can develop really freely and the way nature intended.

Herbs Help Each Other

In the natural garden, a variety of wild herbs are used to defend against garden pests and to ward off diseases. Even several spice plants can profitably be put to such use. In a well-tended herb garden, catastrophes such as those that can occur in a vegetable or fruit garden are relatively rare. The abundance of strongly scented plants draws honeybees and bumblebees in droves, but harmful insects are evidently irritated and driven away by these very same plants.

Attentive organic gardeners have already learned this from experience. Spray solutions made from common wormwood or

tansy, for example, serve as deterrents to lice and mites. For hundreds of years people have been using the strong scents of certain herbs to drive moths, flies, and vermin out of the house. Plants that can be used for such purposes were described and recommended in medieval herb books.

In keeping with an old tradition,

Borage and tarragon need moist soil and a lot of light and space to develop fully.

people today still hang small bouquets of lavender, southernwood, costmary, and tansy in closets and living rooms.

Since many of these fragrant plants grow next to one another in the herb bed, the garden can help itself to a certain extent with these natural methods. But, should a plague of insects or mildew turn up as a result of unfavorable weather conditions or through an error in planting, you can also help yourself with home-made botanical sprays that have no harmful side effects.

Stinging-Nettle—
Cold-Water Extract
Fill a 10-quart plastic bucket or pail with freshly picked stinging nettles (before the plants set their seeds) and fill the pail with water. This brew should be left to steep for 12–24 hours, but it should not be allowed to ferment. The cold-

The Organic Method of . . .

water extract is then sprayed in undiluted concentrations directly over the plants. It is effective against light infestations of leaf lice.

Stinging-Nettle Liquid Manure
Freshly picked (or even dried) stinging nettles should be placed in either a plastic bucket, a stoneware crock, or a wooden pail and covered with water, preferably rainwater. Stir this brew vigorously once a day so that oxygen can mix in with the fermentation process. You can fix the unpleasant odors by tossing a handful of stone meal or a few drops of valerian-blossom extract into the container. In order to prevent birds from drowning in the container, you may want to place a grate over the opening during these early stages. Later, when the liquid manure is ready to be used, you can cover the container with a proper lid.

Your stinging-nettle liquid manure will be especially rich if you mix in a few handfuls of other garden or wild herbs. Suitable for this purpose are chives, comfrey, dandelions, horsetail, tansy, and wormwood.

After 2 or 3 weeks the fermentation process should be completed. For use in the vegetable garden, dilute this liquid manure in the proportions of 1 part to 10 of water. A concentration of 1 part liquid manure to 20 parts water can be used in the herb garden. A generous dose directly onto the root area is sufficient. The liquid

fertilizer made from these wholesome nettles has an overall strengthening effect. It renders the plants resistant from within against diseases and pests.

A diluted solution of this liquid manure can also be used in a kitchen garden as a means to ward off insects. Just spray it on the leaves. Because of the rather unpleasant odor of this brew, it is better not to use it in the herb garden. After all, your lemon balm should taste of lemons and not of liquid manure!

Tansy Tea
Brew up a tea made of 300 grams of fresh tansy (both blossoms and leaves) or 30 grams of the dried herb with 10 quarts of boiling water. Let it steep for 10 to 15

"Caustic liquid manure" is sprayed on plants.

minutes. Sift the solution and dilute it with water after it has cooled, in the proportion of 1 part tea to 3 parts water. This herbal tea can be used as a spray against mites and various vermin as well as against rust and mildew. Tansy tea can also be combined with horsetail tea.

Wormwood Tea

300 grams of fresh wormwood leaves (gathered before the bloom) or 30 grams of the dried herb are brewed with 10 quarts of water. Prepare this solution the same way you prepare the tansy recipe. Wormwood tea should be poured over the plants in undiluted concentrations in the spring; in the summer it should be diluted 1 part tea to 3 parts water. Wormwood tea protects against, among other pests, lice, ants, and caterpillars.

Horsetail Solution

Horsetail is one of the oldest plants known to man, and it grows in many gardens as a weed. The fresh herb should be gathered from May to August, but you can also buy it in dried form, as a powder, or in the form of a liquid extract. For 10 quarts of water you will need 300 grams of fresh or 30 grams of dried herbs.

The first step is to let the horsetail herbs soak in water for 24 hours, after which time you should boil the solution. The brew should continue to simmer at a lower temperature for another 30 minutes or so. Let the whole concoction cool and then pass the liquid through a sieve.

Horsetail solution is diluted 1 part to 5 with water and sprayed over the plants toward the end of a sunny morning. This herbal extract contains a large amount of silicic acid. It strengthens the cells of the plants and thus makes it difficult for fungi to penetrate. This horsetail solution should be used frequently as a prophylactic measure from spring until summer.

Organic Plant Protection with Natural Products

In acute instances several special organic means of plant protection have rapid results. If the time should come when you really

Tansy grows wild or in the garden.

The Organic Method of . . .

have to defend against a critical infestation of lice in your herb garden, you might want to resort, as a last measure, to the following recipe:

Soft-Soap Solution
Dissolve 150–300 grams of pure soft soap (from the drugstore or pharmacy) into 10 quarts of hot water; let the solution cool and then spray it on the affected plants. Soft-soap solutions are very reliable against lice and spider mites, but they are also lethal to useful insects. This is why you should use this liquid only in emergency situations, when the very existence of an herb or of an entire bed is really endangered.

Several organic preparations that can be applied either as a prophylactic or directly against insect pests are also commercially available. For example, pyrethrum preparations can be relied upon to combat lice, mites, or white flies, but they affect the useful insects as well. Other products strengthen the plants' resistance against mildew.

If you tend your herb garden in a sensible and natural way, you will rarely be compelled to resort to direct defensive actions. Be particularly careful when working with any foreign agent in the "Kingdom of Delicate Scents." After all, you do want to enjoy the spicy leaves in an unadulterated form. The longer you work with herbs, the more intensely you will realize that these plants are "special." Their precious ingredients,

Horsetail in summer.

their aroma, and their pleasant fragrances, just like their natural defenses, develop only where the herbs can fully unfold. If you treat them like cabbages, they will wither away in your very hands. And then no spray will do any good.

Organic Tips for Crisis Situations

Under certain unfavorable circumstances, several herbs become susceptible to very specific diseases or insects. The following tips are meant to help you through these crisis situations.

Parsley Wilt
The most beautiful green parsley

plant can collapse overnight; its leaves turn yellow and wilt. Frequently the stems droop as well. If you dig up the affected plant, you will see that the roots show signs of putrefaction or of having been eaten away. There can be various causes for this:

1. *Carrot-rust flies*—their maggots eat their way into the roots. You can recognize them by their brown gangways.
2. *Nematodes*—the roots putrefy and die.

Prophylactic mixed plantings are effective against carrot-rust flies; sow the parsley in alternating rows with chives or onions. You can also water the endangered plants rather frequently with strong-smelling herbal teas made of wormwood or tansy.

The best way to combat nematodes is to disinfect the soil with tagetes and pot marigolds. Sow these attractive flowers at the very spots in the herb bed where you will plant parsley next year. The root secretions of these useful plants drive the harmful nematodes away. If you are not absolutely certain that you have gotten rid of all of these creatures, you can also plant tagetes and parsley in alternating rows.

One additional important tip for healthy parsley: This particular spice plant is incompatible with itself. You should sow it in a different place every year, for if it remains in the same spot for any length of time, it will wilt and wither.

Soft soap and fuel alcohol.

Trouble with Dill

Carrot-rust flies also tend to congregate on the long taproots of the dill plant. If this happens, follow the directions above for the best method of eliminating this pest. Frequently, however, it is not flies but an unfavorable location that is causing the dill to act like an insulted prima donna. Try planting a new crop along the edge of the cucumber bed, for this herb often thrives better there than in the herb garden. The cucumber tendrils with their broad leaves keep the soil moist, and dill roots are especially comfortable in loose humus with uniform moisture. If it then gets a lot of sun on its above-ground parts as well, this herb will flourish gloriously and can easily grow 3′ to 5′ tall. Another tip: When buying

43

The Organic Method of . . .

seeds, pay particular attention to the quality of the variety, to the protective ability of the packaging itself, and to the expiration date.

Peppermint Rust
Peppermint rust, a fungus infection, is caused by a too-close, suffocating environment. Once this disease has reached critical proportions, only a radical cutting back of the plants will do any good. The new shoots are usually healthy again. In order to avoid further damage in the following year, you would do well to improve the growth conditions. Thin the plants out a bit so that they get more light, or give them more lateral space to spread out in. Peppermint also thrives on the edge of a loose hedge or near a pond. Organic tip: Peppermint does not flourish well when planted near camomile.

Ground Fleas on Cress
These small, voracious bugs love *Cruciferae* above all else, and this means they attack cabbage and red and black radishes. They munch ugly holes in the leaves of the young plants, and in many gardens they also attack newly germinated cress.

Make sure that the soil in which your cress is growing remains moist at all times—either through

Parsley and pot marigolds grow in a mixed planting.

regular watering or through a light grass-mulch cover. Ground fleas love dry soil. Branches of blooming broom make a good ground-flea barrier that can surround the plants on all sides. Just place them on the ground in a circle around your cress.

Slugs on Young Seedlings

Many a brand-new row of herbs that have just unfolded their very first tender young leaves above the brown soil falls victim to slugs overnight. These creeping creatures are apparently especially fond of basil, purslane, and sweet marjoram.

Bury several plastic containers (yogurt or dishwashing-soap containers will do nicely) with their rims level with the ground in the places where the newly germinated seedlings are expected to appear. Fill these traps about ⅔ full with beer every evening. Then place another, larger container upside down over each trap, remembering to cut little doorways in the rim. You can attach the covers to the buried traps with a piece of pliable wire, and in this way the beer will not be diluted in rainy weather.

Slugs of all sizes literally dive into this heady brew made of hops and malt and drown. If you empty the traps every evening and refill them with fresh beer, you can keep the nocturnal invasion under control. If your garden is particularly overrun, as, for example, it may be if it borders on open meadows whence ever new

Luxuriant dill on the edge of the cucumber bed.

troops of slugs wander in day and night, you might try spreading a broad strip of coarse sand all around the herb bed or around the whole herb garden, for that matter. These creatures are unable to conquer this obstacle.

You can also strew some powdered stone, lime, or wood ashes around the individual plants or rows of herbs in such broad strips, but these measures help only in dry weather. Several strong-smelling herbs planted in the same garden also exert a cer-

The Organic Method of . . .

tain defensive action against slugs: these include sage, hyssop, and thyme. Unfortunately, this approach is not completely reliable.

Bad Neighbors

Not all medicinal and spice plants are comfortable next to each other. These independent plants with their individual and pronounced fragrances grow in specific places in nature, and thus they choose their own neighbors, as it were. The gardener has to make allowances for such community preferences in his or her garden as well, because there are herbs that just don't get along if they have to live too close to one another. They wither or fall victim

Beer traps catch slugs.

to disease because they cannot tolerate the secretions of their neighbor. To keep your herb garden healthy, you should avoid the following inauspicious combinations:

- caraway and fennel
- peppermint and camomile
  Common wormwood hinders the growth of many plants, and this is why you should plant it as far away as possible.

Several particularly strong and intense-smelling herbs keep pests away from neighboring vegetable plants. This is why they are eagerly included in vegetable beds and ornamental gardens. Other spice plants have a positive effect on the aroma of their neighbors. And, finally, many herbs also play an important supporting role as sources of honey or nectar for bees, butterflies, and other useful insects. This, too, should be kept in mind when you plan the arrangement of spice plants in your garden.

Herbs as Part of a Mixed Planting

Try the following combinations of herbs with vegetables, fruits, or flowers. The observations you will make are much more valuable than any gardening theory.

- *Summer savory* on the edge of the bush-bean bed protects this vegetable from black lice.
- *Peppermint* wards off white cabbage butterflies and ground fleas. It also makes a good bor-

Peppermint should not be planted near camomile.

der for the cabbage patch. One thing to remember, though, is that this plant is a very vigorous grower!

- *Sage* and *thyme* drive away white cabbage butterflies and slugs if planted as a protective hedge all around a bed. They are not 100% reliable, however.
- *Tansy* as an edge plant tends to ward off ants and other vermin.
- *Common nasturtiums* keep woolly lice and black-leaf lice away from fruit trees if sown on the surfaces of tree stumps.
- *Lavender* protects roses against lice.

- *Cress* improves the aroma of radishes when both are planted in alternating rows.
- *Caraway* as an edge plant has a positive effect on the taste of potatoes. Other good neighbors for potatoes are common nasturtiums and horseradish if there is enough room.
- *Dill,* like its related *Umbelliferae* caraway, fennel, and coriander, makes a good neighbor for cucumbers; it also feels right at home in the company of carrots and onions.
- *Parsley* maintains very good relations with tomatoes, but

Herbs Keep the Garden Healthy

this old kitchen spice does not get on well with head lettuce.

You can see that there are many possible arrangements of herbs in a garden to encourage health, flavor, and aroma. Our knowledge about "green neighbors," however, is by no means complete. The examples in this chapter are meant to stimulate your imagination toward your own observations and new experiments. The positive or even negative influences of herbs on their neighboring plants are probably due to their fragrances as well as in part to their root secretions. The better acquainted you become with your spice and medicinal plants, the more you will develop a sense of their individual characteristics and qualities.

A little herbal witchcraft with fragrances and extracts, with compatible or incompatible secretions, will no longer seem improbable to you. What at first sight seems like a gardening miracle is in reality only a hidden natural law just waiting for discovery. Spend some time patiently and lovingly observing your little aromatic world. The magic of herbs will not be lost if you lift the veil of their secrets with a careful gardener's hand.

Herbs as Part of a Bee-and-Butterfly Garden

Butterflies, bumblebees, honeybees, syrphid flies, and many other insects frequently have to make do with very sparse rations

Summer savory next to bush beans.

Nasturtiums attract lice.

Cheerful, colorful flowers such as these can enclose your herb garden.

in nature's wilds. Blooming fields and meadows are to a great extent a thing of the past. Wild sage, field thyme, apple mint, and many other wild herbs that were once the natural sources and reservoirs of honey and nectar have become rare indeed. An herb garden, therefore, represents an enchanting magnet for bees and other insects. They come from all over and far away and "graze" in the abundant blossoms. And as a token of their gratitude they pollinate the gardener's fruit trees. Several of them even lay their eggs on certain vegetable plants, and the larvae that crawl out of the eggs a short time later gobble up large numbers of leaf lice.

Gardeners who apply the organic methods should there-

Good neighbors: lavender and roses
(left) and cress and radishes (below).

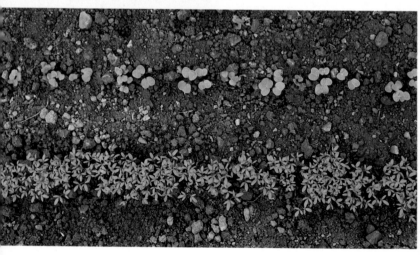

Herbs Keep the Garden Healthy

Blooming borage plants are very popular with bees.

fore consider herbs quite consciously as bee and insect food. If they do this, they will have the satisfaction of knowing that they are working together with nature in a very important area. A portion of the various spice and herb plants should always be allowed to bloom, even if this might mean a decrease in one's crop. The sight of a large borage plant completely covered with sky-blue blossoms and filled with the hum of innumerable bees will richly repay you for this slight loss.

The following plants are particularly popular with bees: borage, lemon balm, and thyme. Even so, sage, hyssop, rosemary, summer savory, wild marjoram, blooming chives, lavender, and mullein also attract these winged honey-collectors.

Herbs belonging to the *Umbellifera* family attract useful syrphid flies: parsley, caraway, and cor-

Harvesting and Preserving

Blooming herbs attract butterflies.

Picking and Putting Up

It pays to preserve your home-grown herbs and to have them handy for use during the winter. They serve as seasonings in the kitchen and make teas that soothe colds or stomach discomforts. Moreover, by preserving fresh herbs in vinegar or oil, you will retain their aroma and their medicinal properties as well.

When and How to Harvest

Every herb reaches maturity at a certain time in the summer or fall. This is when it is especially rich in aroma and medicinal properties. You should thus plan to harvest your spice and medicinal plants during these brief days or weeks. Since every herb grows and ripens according to its own life rhythm, you will have to learn just when the best time to pick has arrived. This information is included in every one of the descriptions of individual herbs later in this book. Meet these harvesting "deadlines" because they signify a guaranty of good quality.

The concentration of valuable ingredients in an herb, however, is dependent upon the weather. The amount of essential oils, for example, is greater in sunny years than after a cool, rainy summer. You can always pick fresh leaves from many of these plants from spring to fall for your daily consumption in the kitchen. This information, too, is included in

iander. Fennel, dill, and caraway are very popular with swallowtails. Peacock butterflies lay their eggs on stinging-nettle shrubs and their larvae later eat the leaves.

These are only a few examples of the diversity of life that makes its home in spice and herb gardens. It hums and buzzes all summer long among the fragrant plants. Attentive gardeners will always find something fascinating to watch here, and these lessons will greatly enhance their understanding of nature.

Harvesting and Preserving

the individual descriptions. It is always best to pick individual small twigs, leaves, or blossoms carefully by hand. Stiffer stalks should be cut off smoothly with a very sharp knife or a pair of rose-clippers. Try to avoid rips and injuries to the plants, because such wounds are open doors for insects and diseases.

Drying Herbs

A great many herbs respond very well to drying and can then be kept for about one year. After that they lose their seasoning and medicinal properties. This method of saving herbs is ancient, but it works just as well today as it did thousands of years

Your summer herb harvest can be preserved in many ways.

Harvesting and Preserving

Herbs can be harvested by hand or with a pair of scissors.

ago. The following plants are only some of the many that can be dried: thyme, wild marjoram, sage, peppermint, camomile, St.-John's-wort, lavender, sweet marjoram, summer savory, mugwort, and wormwood.

It is best to cut the herbs you intend to dry rather late in the morning on a sunny day. The dew of the previous evening should already be gone, but the midday heat should not yet have "exhausted" the leaves.

Gather the cut herbs in a well-ventilated wicker basket, but make sure that they rest only lightly on top of one another. Carefully examine them all again once you get inside, because only unblemished, healthy plants can be put up. Give each branch a rather vigorous shake to dislodge any small insects that may be hidden in it. The ideal method would be to dry your herbs exactly as they were when harvested, but this is not always possible. In areas with air-pollution problems, you will unfortunately have to wash the plants very carefully. Shake off all excess water and carefully pat the leaves dry with a paper towel. Place the herbs on a well-ventilated grate until they are completely dry. Only after the leaves are no longer moist can you proceed with the drying process.

Tie up the different herbs into loose bouquets and hang them upside down on a line. The drying room must be shady and airy. Hot sun is just as harmful as sticky, damp air. Wait until the leaves are

Bouquets of herbs hanging up to dry.

dry enough that they rustle and crackle between your fingers, and then put them in jars or tea canisters. In doing this, remember to rub the leaves and the blossoms off the stems. It is also important to make sure that the containers can be closed and kept airtight, either with a screw cover or a cork. This is the best way to preserve the spice and medicinal properties of the herbs.

If you don't have a drying line, you can lay your herbs very loosely on top of a well-ventilated grate or screen to dry. They can also be put in the drying machines that are meant for fruit and vegetables. Remember to keep the temperature low.

Some medicinal plants offer their roots for harvesting and preserving. Elecampane, common valerian, and angelica are examples of such plants. This usually happens in the fall or in the spring. Using a spade or a sharp knife, cut off only as many pieces of root as the plant can afford to lose without danger. These brown, fleshy portions should be carefully cleaned of excess dirt, brushed under running water, and rubbed dry. Cut the large roots into pieces, but leave the smaller pieces whole. You can use a darning needle and a strong string to join the roots together on a piece of twine and, like the herb bouquets, hang them up to dry.

55

Harvesting and Preserving

These do-it-yourself drying racks are constructed of wooden frames and window screening.

There are still other spice plants from which you can harvest the seeds. Caraway, coriander, and tea fennel belong to this group. These herbs have to be observed closely during the harvest period. Cut off the blossoms with the seeds shortly before they ripen, because if you do not, they can easily loosen and fall.

Tie these seed herbs together in loose bunches, too, and hang them up to dry, but spread a cotton towel or some kitchen shelving paper underneath them. This is where you will collect the ripe and fallen seeds. As a last step you should strike the bunches against the paper or towel rather vigorously. You will remove the

Commercially available drying machines with several sieves and temperature regulator.

leaves and dust when you shake the seeds in a fine sieve or colander. The light chaff will remain on top and can be discarded. You should store your seed crop, just as you did your leaves, flowers, and roots, in closed containers.

Preserving Herbs in Vinegar or Oil

One of the oldest and most honored ways of preserving herbs is to put them up in vinegar or oil. These products have preserving qualities that hinder the activities of harmful bacteria. After a while the aroma and the medicinal qualities of the herbs are transferred to the fluid. This is how vinegar and oil become the bearers of spice and medicinal substances.

The preparation requires but little work and effort. Clean and dry the appropriate parts of the plants and put them in clean, dry bottles. Remember to distribute them loosely enough so that the filled containers can be shaken easily and the substances can be thoroughly mixed.

Now pour the vinegar or oil over the herbs. The entire piece must be completely covered, because if a leaf or a stem pokes out, you risk putrefaction. For these preparations you should use a good wine vinegar and virgin olive oil. Other vegetable oils can also be used.

Cork the bottles tightly and place them on a sunny, warm win-

Dried herbs are removed from the stems and crumbled.

dowsill. From now on they should be shaken vigorously once a day. The herbed vinegar should be ready to use in 2 to 3 weeks, and it can be stored in a dark place for years. The herbed oils need 3 to 6 weeks before they are ready to be filtered. The best way to do this is to pour the liquid through a clean handkerchief lining a large funnel. When you have poured it all, squeeze the handkerchief tightly to make sure that all the valuable ingredients end up in the bottle. Herbed oil should be stored in a cool and dark place in a brown or green bottle.

Herbed oils should be left on a sunny windowsill for several weeks.

The following herbs make very good herbed vinegars, either by themselves or in groups: tarragon, dill, lemon balm, basil, and nasturtiums. For herbed oils you can use, among others, sweet marjoram, thyme, southernwood, sage, rosemary, peppermint, dill, lavender, garlic, and St-John's-wort (see the recipe, p. 62).

Freezing Herbs

Modern methods of freezing have proven to be very good for many varieties of vegetables and fruits, but this ice-cold preserving process is less appropriate for the more sensitive herbs. What usually remains after thawing them is a wilted pile of wet misery that has hardly any aroma left. This method pays off in only very few cases.

You can freeze fresh dill leaves in small portions. Parsley is another herb that does not suffer, but just about any method of preserving is unnecessary in this case, because parsley remains green and fresh all winter long. You can freeze a few stalks of summer savory together with your green beans, and it is worth a try to freeze a few pieces of celery for your winter stews.

When you prepare herbs for freezing, pack up only as much as will be needed for one dish at a time, because once you thaw these plants they cannot be kept very long.

Harvesting and Preserving

Fresh Herbs in the Winter

You can do yourself and your family a vitamin-rich kindness by serving fresh green herbs during the long winter months. This is why smart gardeners always sow sufficiently early all those spice plants that remain green even beneath a layer of snow. Parsley, scurvy grass, and bitter winter cress are among these evergreen herbs. In mild winters even a few leaves of salad burnet, garden sorrel, and winter purslane remain alive. If you place a few pine branches on top of these herbs, you will be able to harvest them in the snow.

The most important thing to remember is to plan ahead. If you plant a chive ball that has been hit by frost in late autumn and put it on a bright, not too warm windowsill, it will develop spicy green stalks over the winter.

Basil, too, that has been planted in a flower pot will thrive for a while on a warm windowsill and produce spicy leaves for the kitchen. Especially easy and successful is the sowing of cress. Sprinkle the seeds on a piece of damp paper toweling that you have spread out on a plate or dish. Small pots filled with wet sand also make good rooting ground for this modest herb. Cress germinates so rapidly you can almost watch it grow. Only 8 to 10 days later you can harvest that spicy green plant with its typical, somewhat sharp cress taste. To an herb gardener who com-

White and red wine vinegar with herbs.

Frozen herbs.

59

Harvesting and Preserving

bines imagination with timely provisions for the future, the winter, too, remains at least a partially green season.

How to Make the Most of the Taste

This is an herb-garden book. Its main purpose is to help you in setting up and caring for the spice and medicinal plants in your own garden. The use of fresh or dried herbs in the kitchen is a topic that could fill many another volume. Similarly, the preparation of medicinal teas or homemade oils, tinctures, and salves for the medicine chest is a science in itself. You can study these things in the voluminous literature that is available in every good bookstore.

All I want to do here is introduce you to a small selection of recipes. Use them as a source of inspiration for your own experiments and further reading. The following examples are only meant to start you on your way. I am confident that, once you have tasted these dainties, you will never want to leave this fragrant, tasty "sorcerer's kitchen."

Cress seedlings in decorative clay pots, on saucers, and in plastic containers. Above: soaking seeds.

Harvesting and Preserving

Recipes for the Kitchen

Colorful Summer Salad
Combine head lettuce or iceberg lettuce with fresh cucumber slices and pieces of tomato. To make the marinade, stir 3 tablespoons of good vegetable oil in with 1 tablespoon of wine vinegar. Season with salt, a little pepper, and a small clove of garlic. Then add 1 or 2 handfuls of fresh, finely chopped herbs of the season. The following combinations go well together:

- chives, borage, salad burnet, and lemon balm
- borage, dill, and lemon balm
- stonecrop, salad burnet, tarragon, borage, southernwood, and hyssop
- basil and lemon balm

Mix the fresh herbs into the marinade and add a little sweet or sour cream according to taste. Shortly before you serve it, pour the dressing over the mixed salad and decorate it with blue borage blossoms, daisies, and nasturtium blossoms.

Basil Chicken
Carefully season a young chicken with salt and pepper and stuff it with fresh basil branches. Add a small glassful of wine and roast the chicken in a clay pot. The distinctive basil taste will seep into the whole chicken and result in an incomparable taste. Use the drippings to make a light gravy and season it with a few additional finely chopped basil leaves

and a little wine or sherry. Serve this dish with green noodles or rice.

Herbed Roast with Pears
Rub salt and pepper into a pork roast and place it in a wet clay pot on top of a bed of sage leaves, thyme, wild marjoram, and sweet marjoram. You can also sprinkle some fresh or dried sprigs of herbs on top of the meat. Then place peeled pear quarters all around the roast, but make sure they are absolutely fresh pears. The brown, spicy winter pears taste best. The juices from the meat, the herbs, and the fruit together produce a delicious aroma. You can serve the drippings as they are or use them to make a light gravy. Potatoes or rice goes well with this dish.

Springtime variations with violet blossoms.

Harvesting and Preserving

Recipes for Medicinal Purposes

Red St. John's Oil

The blossoms as well as the leaves of St.-John's-wort should be picked toward the end of June (Midsummer Day), carefully sorted out, and put in bottles. Make sure you check to see that the leaves show small bright spots when you hold them up to the light. These pinpoint "perforations" are the distinguishing characteristic of genuine St.-John's-wort. All the other varieties of this plant are without any medicinal value.

Cover the leaves and the blossoms with virgin olive oil of the best quality and close the bottle tightly. It is important that the herbs should be completely covered by the oil. This solution has to stand on a warm, sunny windowsill for 5 to 6 weeks. Shake the bottle vigorously every day. The contents should begin to gradually turn red. When the process is finished, genuine St. John's oil is a bright blood-red color. It should now be filtered through a clean handkerchief. Squeeze the remaining "leftovers" in the handkerchief so that all the valuable ingredients remain in the oil. Store this red oil in a cool and dark place; it can be used to heal minor burns and sunburn, and you can massage it into muscles sore with rheumatism. Internally, St. John's oil is said to help relieve nervousness and light depression.

Lavender Oil

The blue blossoms of the lavender plant can also be covered with olive oil or a good vegetable oil. And, just like St. John's oil, it should be left on a warm windowsill for 3 to 4 weeks, after which it should be filtered. This fragrant lavender oil helps alleviate headaches and sore nerves if you rub it on. It can also be added to the bathwater.

Stuffing with large-leafed basil.

Recipes for Everyday Use

Herbs for Insect Bites

Fresh herbs from the garden lessen the pain of a bee sting or bug bite if they are applied immediately. Crush them between your fingers until the sap runs and then use the leaf to rub on the bite. You can also let the leaves lie on the small wound for a little while to continue their effect. The stinger, of course, must always be removed first! The following herbs can be used for this home-made first-aid remedy: lemon balm, costmary, ribwort, and fresh onion juice. The pain disappears quickly, and swelling is usually prevented.

Sage Tea for Sore Throats
The silver-gray leaves of the sage plant have a slightly contracting effect. They are an excellent remedy for sore-throat pains. For 1 cup of tea you will need 1 teaspoonful of dried sage. Pour hot water over this, cover the brew, and let it steep for 5 to 10 minutes.

Sweeten with honey and drink this sharp and spicy tea slowly, one swallow at a time. Once it has cooled off somewhat, you can use it unsweetened as a gargle.

A Cough Remedy from the Herb Garden
This tea mixture dissolves congestions, frees the bronchia and strengthens the body's resistance: mix equal amounts of thyme, mullein blossoms, mallow blossoms, and violet blossoms. This cough remedy should be brewed exactly the same way as sage tea. Sweeten it with honey and drink it slowly 2 to 3 times a day until your cold is gone.

St. John's oil after 2 and after 6 weeks.

Herbal Sachets Against Moths and Flies
During the summertime you can hang bouquets of tansy, wormwood, and southernwood in the living room of your home or apartment. They will keep flies and vermin away. Even if this herbal protection is not 100% effective, it does represent a more pleasant way of getting rid of bothersome insects than poisonous sprays.

To combat moths, you can tie up small bunches of herbs and, once they are dried, pack them into small cotton sachets and hang them in closets or put them in drawers. You can use, either individually or in combination, lavender blossoms, southernwood, and costmary. Their pleasant scent will accompany you for a long time in your clothes and bed linens.

Introducing the Herbs

The following pages describe the most important spice and medicinal herbs that you can cultivate in your garden. The individual descriptions are arranged according to their relationship within the larger botanical families. The accompanying illustrations are meant to serve as a guide as well as a visual supplement to the text.

The various portraits contain information about the origin, the appearance, and the characteristics of the plants; these are followed by tips concerning cultivation in the garden, the most auspicious time to harvest, and the best methods of preserving the herbs. Additional information about the taste, use as a seasoning, and medicinal properties of these herbs can be found in the tables starting on p. 118.

Let's start with the basics for a kitchen garden. Annual and biennial herbs have to be replanted from seed every year. Perennial herbs remain in the same location from one year to the next. They set new shoots in the spring from rhizomes or from woody branches. You should combine short-lived and more durable spicy and medicinal herbs in a varied mixed planting. The more herbs with which you become personally acquainted, the richer will be your harvest of these special plants.

Sage tea from your own garden.

Introducing the Herbs

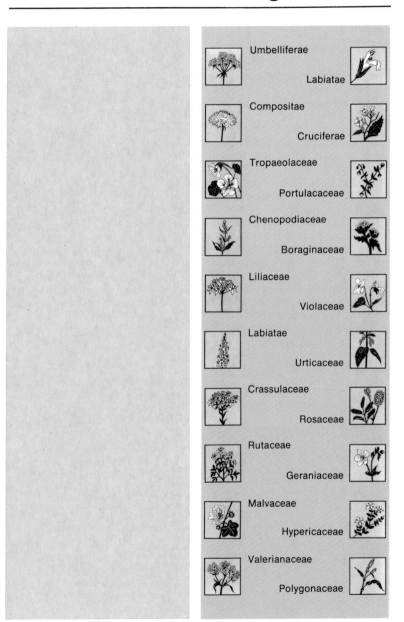

Umbelliferae

Labiatae

Compositae

Cruciferae

Tropaeolaceae

Portulacaceae

Chenopodiaceae

Boraginaceae

Liliaceae

Violaceae

Labiatae

Urticaceae

Crassulaceae

Rosaceae

Rutaceae

Geraniaceae

Malvaceae

Hypericaceae

Valerianaceae

Polygonaceae

Anise
(Pimpinella anisum)

Origin: Anise is indigenous to the eastern regions of the Mediterranean. It was well known in ancient times and highly prized by the Romans. During the Middle Ages this herb with its sweet but spicy seeds also flourished in European cloister gardens.

Botanical Description: Anise is a member of the *Umbellifera* family. This plant drives a long, slender taproot deep into the soil and forms a rosette of leaves close to the ground. Out of this rosette grows a grooved stalk which can reach a height of 12″ to 19″. Three different types of leaves develop on this stalk: the lowest leaves are smooth, the ones in the middle region are pinnate with 3 to 5 sections, and the uppermost leaves on the stalk are very narrow and deeply denticulated. Anise produces white, umbrellalike clumps of blossoms from July to August. The individual seeds lie in pairs in small, egg-shaped fruits.

Cultivation: Anise needs soil rich in humus and a warm, sunny location. In cold, wet summers the seeds frequently fail to ripen. Plant this aromatic herb in open beds from April onward. The rows should be about 8″ to 12″ apart, and it can take up to 4 weeks before the seed germinates. The young plants can be thinned out later to about 5″ apart to ensure a good growth.

Dill
(Anethum graveolens)

Origin: Dill is believed to come from southeastern Europe and the Far East. It ranks among the oldest spice and medicinal herbs and was under wide cultivation as far back as the days of Charlemagne.

Botanical Description: Dill is a member of the *Umbellifera* family, and it forms a long taproot. The stem is hollow and the pinnate leaves surround it with their leaf sheaths. These plants are crowned by radiated yellow blossom clusters from June to August. The pods are round and elongated, and each one contains 2 seeds. The shape of the dill plant resembles that of fennel, but it is somewhat more delicate.

Cultivation: You can plant dill in open beds from April onward. This herb likes a uniformly moist

Anise

Dill

humus soil, but it has to be loose and porous. The above-ground parts need a lot of sun. The rows should be about 10" to 12" apart. Once they have developed their long taproots, though, these plants should not be transplanted. It is better to thin them out when it seems necessary. Reseed once or twice, in order to ensure a long and fresh harvest. You will need a lot of dill once you start to preserve other crops. If the conditions are right, this aromatic herb can grow to a height of 5'.

Mulch covers composed of grass keep the soil moist in the summertime. Dill also thrives well when planted between cucumber runners.

Harvesting and Preserving: You can pick fresh dill leaves from early summer until the beginning of fall. The blossoms containing the dill seeds should be dried when they turn brown in the fall.

You can even use the blossoms when preserving pickles. Green dill can be frozen at any time.

Chervil
(Anthriscus cerefolium)

Origin: Chervil is native to southern Europe and western Asia, whence it found its way into the regions surrounding the Mediterranean. It is highly probable that Roman legions brought this herb across the Alps.

Botanical Description: Chervil, too, is a member of the *Umbelliferae,* and is related to carrots and parsley. A tall, grooved stalk develops from thin, spindle-shaped roots. The plants branch out and form light green, pinnate leaves with 3 to 4 sections. Long stems grow out of the leaf axils, and the tips of these stems are crowned with delicate white flower clusters from May to August.

Chervil

67

Annual Herbs

Cultivation: Chervil is not a sensitive herb and it can thus be planted as early as May if the weather permits. The rows should be about 4″ apart. Sow the seeds sparingly, because it does not pay to transplant these herbs. Chervil likes light shade and a rather moist soil; in all other respects it is undemanding.

Chervil grows rapidly and is ready to be picked after only a few weeks. However, it also blooms very quickly. If you like this herb, you should plant new rows frequently. You can choose between smooth-leafed varieties and those with curly leaves.

Harvesting and Preserving: Only the freshly picked young herb tastes good and spicy. In any case, you should cut it before it blooms. Preserving is not worth the effort; the best you can do is "harvest" a few seeds for next year's crop.

Coriander
(Coriandrum sativum)

Origin: Coriander is at home along the Mediterranean and in the Middle East. It has been used for centuries in India, China, Egypt, and the Orient. The Romans brought this herb over the Alps and into northern Europe.

Botanical Description: Coriander is another member of the *Umbellifera* family. It has the typical spindle-shaped root and grooved stalks. These plants, too,

branch out and form 2 different types of leaves: the lower leaves are 3-pronged, the upper ones delicately pinnate. Pinkish-white blossom clusters unfold on the tips of the stems from June to July. The round seeds consist of 2 hemispheres.

Cultivation: You can plant coriander in open beds as early as April. It prefers a loose, somewhat limy soil and direct sun. The seeds should be planted about ⅓″

Coriander plants; below, blossoms and seeds.

to ½" deep, and the rows should be about 12" apart. As with all plants with long, thin roots, transplanting is not recommended. Rather than that, you should thin the rows out so that there is about 3" to 5" between the individual plants. This herb is otherwise very undemanding; depending upon the location, it can grow to a height of 1' to 2'.

Harvesting and Preserving:
Usually, only the seeds of the coriander plant are used. Cut the blossoms just before they become dry, brown, and ripe, for if you do not catch them in time, the seeds will easily fall to the ground. Remember to cut the stems long enough to be able to tie the bunches together for drying. The green leaves have a unique smell which is said to be reminiscent of bugbane. Nevertheless, they are used in plentiful amounts in the Orient. Try some and see if you like them.

squarrose, grooved stalk. The pinnate leaves are shiny dark green and the small white blossoms form loose clusters.

Cultivation: Celery should be planted no earlier than May. It is one of the plants that germinate in light; this is why the seeds should be covered with only a very thin layer of soil. You can also force this herb in pots and plant it in the open starting from the middle of May.

Celery grows in the sun as well as in partial shade. It needs a good, nutrient-containing soil and a lot of moisture. Give this sturdy herb some organic fertilizer; the best procedure would be to spread it early in spring as a reserve. Let this herb simply grow in its row, only thinning out the thickest clusters. There should be about 7½" to 8" between the rows.

Celery can tolerate a dose of stinging-nettle liquid manure in the summer. You should also remember to give it ample water

Celery
(Apium graveolens)

Origin: The original wild form of celery is indigenous to the salty soils of the coastal areas of Europe as well as in western Asia, Africa, and South America.

Botanical Description: Celery belongs to the *Umbellifera* family. Unlike the familiar garden vegetables, celery does not form any tubers. The multibranched, spindle-shaped root gives rise to a

Celery

Annual Herbs

during dry spells. Once in a while you might also want to add 1 or 2 tablespoons of cooking salt to the water. This additional nutrient is perfectly natural for celery, since it originates in salty soils.

Harvesting and Preserving: You can harvest fresh leaves continuously as soon as the plants are big enough, but be sure to pick only the young green ones, for the older parts of the plant become leathery and hard. You can dry or freeze celery at any time during the summer.

Sweet Basil

Sweet Basil
(Ocimum basilicum)

Origin: The original home of the basil plant is probably somewhere in the tropical regions of far India. Even so, this herb has been growing in the Orient as well as all along the Mediterranean for thousands of years.

Botanical Description: Basil is a member of the *Labiata* family. The individual plants consist of many branches, and whereas the stalks are squarrose, the leaves are elongated oval in shape and slightly arched. The tips of the stems produce blossoms ranging in color from ivory to pink from July to September. These blossoms, in turn, produce false whorls. Depending upon the climatic conditions, basil can grow to a height of 6″ to 2 ′. Different varieties of this herb are available; one with red leaves grows in Italy.

Cultivation: You have your choice between basil with small and basil with large leaves. The daintier variety has a more delicate aroma; the larger variety, on the other hand, is more resistant.

You can plant this sensitive herb any time between March and April on a warm windowsill or in a greenhouse. Basil needs light to germinate, so the seeds should lie very close to the surface of the ground; they germinate very rapidly. Transplant the young specimens in bunches into small clay or peat pots. Here they may be buried a bit more deeply into the soil so that they can take hold.

Starting about the middle of May, you can plant your basil in a warm and protected spot in an open bed. This herb loves a slightly sandy soil rich in humus, and it has to be watered frequently during dry spells. Keep a distance of about 10″ in all directions. If you remove the central stem, the plants will branch out better. It always pays to plant a few basil bushes in large pots, for this herb thrives better on the windowsill than in the garden during cool and rain-drenched summers. It also looks very pretty there and wards off bothersome flies with its scent.

Harvesting and Preserving: Fresh, young leaves can be picked at any time for use in the kitchen. Older leaves have a somewhat sharper taste. You can also dry basil before it blooms, but it usually loses the greater part of its delicate and spicy aroma. It is a better idea to keep a flower pot with fresh basil on your windowsill all year round.

Summer Savory
(Satureia hortensis)

Origin: Savory is indigenous to the Mediterranean region and was used by the Romans as a strong and spicy herb. It was brought over the Alps and introduced to central Europe in the 9th century by wandering monks.

Botanical Description: Savory is another member of the *Labiatae*. This plant forms a strong main root and multibranched stems. The narrow, dark green leaves are slightly hairy. Small pink, white, or pale violet blossoms develop in the leaf axils from July to August, and they form false spikes.

Cultivation: You can sow savory in a hotbed or under plastic tunnels as early as April, but from May onward it also flourishes in the open. This herb likes warm, loose humus. The rows should be 8" to 10" apart. If you prefer to have multibranched, small bushes, move the young plants about 10" to 12" apart. Savory, too, needs light to germinate, and so the fine seeds should be only lightly covered with soil. If you reseed this herb in early June, you will always have fresh, spicy supplies on hand. If it has taken hold well, savory can even tolerate dry spells. This plant grows to a height of 12" to 15".

Harvesting and Preserving: Fresh leaves and branches can be picked at any time. The aroma is strongest shortly before and again during the bloom; this is the time to cut the savory, tie it in bundles, and hang it up to dry. It retains its spiciness exceptionally well.

Summer Savory

Annual Herbs

Sweet Marjoram
(Majorana hortensis)

Origin: Sweet marjoram is at home in all the countries surrounding the Mediterranean. In its native habitat it grows in the form of small, perennial bushes. In ancient times this herb was used by the Egyptians, the Greeks, and the Romans. It is said to have arrived in the lands north of the Alps toward the end of the Middle Ages.

Botanical Description: Sweet marjoram is a member of the *Labiata* family. It grows into dainty, branched plants with squarrose, slightly hairy stalks. The typical leaves are small, grayish-green, oval, and hairy and possess numerous glands. From June to September roundish flowers that look like long buds appear on the tops of the branches. Pink or white blossoms hide between the green, involucral leaves.

Cultivation: Sweet marjoram can be planted in an open bed from May onward as soon as the soil is warm and loose, but you can begin to force it on the windowsill as early as March or April. In the open garden this herb needs a very sunny location and a porous soil rich in humus. The seeds of the sweet marjoram plant are very delicate; they may be covered with a very thin layer of soil at the most. The rows should be 7½" to 9½" apart. Position the young plants in bunches about 6" apart. If it has taken a strong hold, sweet marjoram is able to survive dry spells. Always make sure that the soil is loose. Under good care this herb can attain a height of 12" to 15".

Harvesting and Preserving: Fresh sprigs can be picked from early summer until late fall, as long as the plants are large enough. If you want to dry it, you should cut the sweet marjoram shortly before the round buds open. Very frequently a second crop will ripen during the warm weeks of Indian summer. This herb retains its intense spicy qualities for a long time. You can also put it up in oil.

Camomile
(Matricaria chamomilla)

Origin: Camomile originally stems from southern Europe; today it is widespread throughout Europe as a wild-growing herb with many varieties.

Sweet Marjoram

Annual Herbs

Botanical Description: Camomile grows into multibranched plants with delicately pinnate leaves; it is a member of the *Composita* family. From June until September the ends of the stems produce flowers with white petals on the edge and yellow, tubular flowers in the middle. In the genuine camomile plant, the outer white petals fold back after fertilization. An important characteristic: If you break open the center of a blossom, you will notice a hollow space tapering downward. If it has not fallen victim to herbicides, genuine camomile likes to grow in wheat fields and along the edges of fields and paths. Scentless camomile and field camomile have no medicinal properties.

Cultivation: You can plant camomile as early as April in rows about 12" to 15" apart, either as a border enclosing a garden bed or simply in random arrangements. The seeds are available in commercial garden centers, and the plants themselves are undemanding. They thrive best in slightly loamy soils rich in humus and in direct sunlight, for this is where the conditions are similar to those in a wheatfield. If the individual plants are too close together, they can be thinned out so that there is at least 8" of free space between them. This will allow them to branch out undisturbed. Camomile grows to a height of 8" to 20".

Harvesting and Preserving: The blossoms should be gathered regularly throughout the blooming season, but only in sunny

Camomile

weather. Dry them carefully and slowly on well-ventilated grates (do not use metal racks or screens). The blossoms must be spread out loosely and may not be on top of one another.

Pot Marigold
(Calendula officinalis)

Origin: Pot marigolds are indigenous to Asia and the southern European countries bordering on the Mediterranean. They made their way across the Alps very early on and were a frequent inhabitant of the farmers' and the cloister gardens of the Middle Ages.

Botanical Description: Pot marigolds are members of the *Composita* family. They have squarrose, multibranched stems that break easily. This results in the oozing out of a sticky sap that has a strong and resinous smell. The elongated leaves are hairy. Yellow or orange radiated blossoms appear on the tips of these stems from June until the first frost.

Cultivation: This ancient medicinal plant and rural garden flower requires little care. It loves direct sunlight and nutrient-containing, somewhat loamy soil, but it also thrives in less favorable locations. The large, curved seeds can be planted in the open garden as early as March. It is best to sow them broadcast and to transplant the seedlings later on with about 8″ to 12″ between the individual plants. Pot marigolds do not need any particular attention. Deep shade and a too crowded location are the only things to guard against. If you continue to remove the withered blossoms, the blooming period lasts that much longer. These plants reseed themselves in the late summer. They usually remain true to the garden for years on end, without the gardener ever needing to reseed them. In an herb or medicinal garden, pot marigolds glow like radiant reflections of the sun.

Harvesting and Preserving: You can pick very young green leaves and blossoms throughout the summer and add them to your salad dishes. The outermost petals can be plucked from freshly unfolding blossoms and carefully and loosely arranged on grids to dry. You can also pour oil over these flower petals.

Pot Marigold

Garden Pepper Cress
(Lepidium sativum)

Origin: The natural habitat of cress was originally somewhere in the Far East, but this herb has been known in the regions north of the Alps ever since the days of Charlemagne.

Botanical Description: Cress belongs to the family of the *Cruciferae*. Multibranched bluish-green stalks grow out of a long, thin taproot. The lower leaves are oval and elongated, while the upper ones are variously pinnate. Small white blossoms appear on the tips of the stalks. The reddish-brown seeds are enclosed in small pods.

Cultivation: Cress is another undemanding herb. You can distribute the seeds in open beds as early as March, and the rows should be about 4″ apart. Cress germinates rapidly and grows in spurts. If you use a lot of this herb, it is best to reseed a new row every 2 to 3 weeks. The leaves become sharp and unappetizing as soon as the plant sets its flowers. It must be watered generously during dry spells; in all other respects, cress is a very undemanding plant. Equally suitable for its cultivation are sunny or partially shady locations.

Harvesting and Preserving: Always cut the fresh, young leaves as long as the herb continues to produce them. There is no need to put any of them up, since you can reseed cress at any time, even during the winter months.

Common Nasturtium
(Tropaeolum majus)

Origin: The plant known as common nasturtium is indigenous to Peru; Spanish conquerors introduced it to Europe.

Botanical Description: Nasturtiums are members of the *Tropaeolacea* family. Long, sap-filled runners grow above short roots, and these runners are covered with shield-shaped leaves. One of the characteristics of this plant is the waxlike coating or crust, which gathers the dew and holds it in the form of glittering spheres

on the leaves. The leaves themselves range in color from pale green to bluish green. The bell-shaped and spurred blossoms glow in warm shades of yellow, orange, and red, and they continue to set new buds right up until the first frost.

Cultivation: Nasturtiums are sensitive to frost. You can begin to force the seeds on the windowsill starting in April and can plant them outdoors starting in May. The large seeds are easy to distribute evenly. Place them about ½″ deep in the soil with a distance

Blooming cress plants—they will soon produce seeds.

of about 4″ between individuals. The climbing variety of nasturtium (*T. majus*) needs a lot of room, for it can also climb up fences and similar grates.

Tropaeolum nanum, on the other hand, forms round, "civilized" bushes. The colorful nasturtiums from Peru love a not too heavy soil rich in humus. They flourish in direct sunlight as well as in partial shade. In an herb garden these plants add cheerful touches of color among the many green leaves of the other plants. This herb is also quite content to grow in pots or tubs on a terrace or balcony.

Harvesting and Preserving: Tender, young leaves can be picked from early summer to late fall. The flowers themselves are not only very decorative but edible as well, and you can put up both flowers and leaves in vinegar. Buds and young seed pods can be preserved in vinegar and used as a substitute for capers.

Common Nasturtium

Purslane
(*Portulaca oleracea*)

Origin: Purslane is another familiar herb that is native to the Far East. Exactly when it made its way to the Mediterranean regions is not known but was certainly early on, and its introduction into northern Europe soon followed. It is described as "rumpweed' in the herb books of the later Middle Ages.

Botanical Description: Purslane is a member of the *Portulacacea* family. It drives a spindle-shaped, branched root deep into the earth. The above-ground portions consist of thick, branched stalks with a greenish-red color. The inverted, oval leaves are likewise fleshy and rich in sap. Small yellow flowers appear on the tips of the stems between the leaves.

Cultivation: The delicate seeds of this warmth-loving herb should not be sown before May. The bed should lie in direct sunlight, and the best soil is a porous, somewhat sandy one. Cover the seeds with a very thin layer of sifted compost. The rows should be about 8″ apart. These plants can be allowed to grow in dense clumps, like spinach, or they can be thinned out to encourage the formation of branches. In the latter case they can attain a height of about 12″. Purslane needs a lot of water to develop its succulent leaves. It can also be reseeded frequently in order to ensure a constant supply of fresh herbs.

Purslane

Harvesting and Preserving:
Purslane grows very rapidly, and only the young, succulent leaves should be harvested. They do not lend themselves to preservation; the most you can do is plant a few specimens in flower pots and put them on the windowsill for the winter.

Winter Purslane
(Montia perfoliata)

Origin: Cuban spinach, another name for winter purslane, is native to America.
Botanical Description: This herb is a member of the *Portulacacea* family. Like lamb's-lettuce *(Valerianella olitoria),* winter purslane forms a "nest" of leaves, which are partly elongated and pointed, partly round like small plates. In the springtime, small, white, star-shaped blossoms grow on tiny stems that emerge from the depression in the middle of the leaf.
Cultivation: April is the earliest you can plant winter purslane in the garden. The delicate seeds should have only a light cover of soil, and the rows should be about 6" apart. Like lamb's-lettuce, you can sow the seeds rather haphazardly so that the herb covers the bed like a carpet. Remember to keep the soil very moist at all times; this is the only demand that this otherwise modest plant makes. Thin out those spots where the growth is too dense in order to make room for the others to develop vigorously.

Winter purslane can be reseeded into already harvested beds from August to September, for this herb will remain green all year long. Nevertheless, it does have to be protected with a covering of either pine or spruce branches. It is also frequently recommended that winter purslane be planted in a hotbed or in an unheated greenhouse in the fall. If the weather is mild, this herb will continue to grow throughout the winter in this type of protected location.
Harvesting and Preserving: You can pick the fresh, young leaves at any time of the year, for they will frequently grow back. Even those leaves adorned with flowers are edible. Preserving does not pay, however, because winter purslane is an evergreen herb.

In the fall, winter purslane resembles field lettuce; in the spring, white blossoms appear in the middle of the leaves.

Orach
(Atriplex hortensis)

Origin: Orach is probably native to Asia, but it found its way to Europe a very long time ago, for Charlemagne left instructions for it to be included in his garden plants. It is one of the oldest herbs in a kitchen garden.

Botanical Description: Orach is a member of the *Chenopodiacea* family. It forms long, branched stalks and characteristically arrow-shaped leaves. These leaves are green and covered with a floury or mealy coating. There is also a cultivar that is wine red in color. Inconspicuous greenish flower clusters grow on stems that emerge from the upper-leaf axils in the summer.

Cultivation: Orach is not sensitive to cold. It can be sown in open beds starting in March or April. Plant the seeds about ⅓″ in the ground, but leave at least 12″ between individual specimens because these herbs branch out strongly and can grow to a height of 4′ to 6′.

Orach flourishes just about anywhere, but it thrives particularly well in moist humus and direct sunlight. These plants produce many seeds and reseed themselves for the most part. The red-leafed variety is particularly attractive in an herb garden, for it provides a colorful contrast to the other foilage.

Harvesting and Preserving: Young, succulent leaves can be picked for the salad bowl throughout the summer, but this herb does not respond well to preserving.

Common Borage
(Borago officinalis)

Origin: Borage is probably indigenous to the Mediterranean regions. The Arabs brought it to Spain, and from there it made its way to central Europe.

Green orach.

Red orach adds color to the herb garden.

Botanical Description: Borage is a member of the *Boraginacea* family. It drives strong roots deep into the earth, and the above-ground portions of the plant are widely branched. The stalks are covered with coarse hairs and are very succulent. Both sides of the elliptical leaves are covered with a hairy surface, which is in keeping with the meaning of the family name. The young leaves feel velvety and succulent, whereas the older leaves are hard and rough to the touch. All summer long, borage produces light blue, sometimes even pink or white, star-shaped blossoms on the tips of the stems.

Cultivation: You can plant the large, squarish borage seeds in the open garden from April onward. This herb germinates in darkness, so you must be sure to cover the seeds well with soil. Do not plant them in rows, but rather strew them about over as large an area as possible; later on you can thin out those clumps that are growing too close together. Borage grows into vigorous, widely branched plants that need a lot of room. If the conditions are right, these plants can attain a height of 2½′ or more. If they are too cramped, there is always the danger of mildew and lice. Young plants do not transplant easily, for the long, thin taproot has difficulty in reestablishing itself.

These vigorous and succulent herbs need a moist, nutrient-containing soil rich in humus. They respond very well to a dose of liquid manure made from stinging nettles. Moreover, a good deal of light and air is essential for healthy growth. If it is comfortable where it is, borage will grow like a weed. It reseeds itself and wanders all over the garden, so it is very important to make sure that your borage does not crowd out other, more tender plants. Soft, young leaves continuously form in the leaf axils of the borage plant. If you reseed a few times a year, you will never run out.

Annual Herbs

Common Borage

Harvesting and Preserving:
Fresh, velvety leaves can be picked when needed, but you have to use them right away because they wilt quickly. The blue flowers are also edible and make a very attractive decoration in the salad bowl. Borage is not worth the trouble it takes to put it up; the most you can do is try to freeze it.

Garlic
(*Allium sativum*)

Origin: Garlic is most probably indigenous to central Asia, but it has been naturalized in many parts of the world for centuries: China, Japan, India, Egypt, Greece, and Italy.
Botanical Description: As a member of the *Liliacea* family, garlic is closely related to onions,

scallions, and leeks. In a strict sense it is not an herb at all, but since it has served as a spice and a medicinal plant since ancient times, it deserves a place in every herb garden.

Garlic consists of a main bulb that is surrounded by slightly curved secondary bulbs, the so-called cloves. The entire bulb is wrapped in a dry, paperlike peel that is either white, pink, or purple in color. The roots grow out of the bottom of the garlic bulb. The above-ground portions of the plant consist of narrow, arched leaves and round flower stems that grow 1' to 3' tall. The pinkish-white, spherical flower is surrounded by an involucral leaf. In addition to the for-the-most-part sterile blossoms, this plant also produces numerous small brood bulbs.

Cultivation: Garlic needs a nutrient-containing garden soil rich in humus but not freshly fertilized. Choose an open, sunny location, and plant the individual cloves about 1½" in the ground. There should be about 6" free space between plants, and the rows should be about 7½" apart.

You have your choice between two optimal planting schedules: March to April or October. The early planting ripens in August, rather parallel to the other onions in your garden, whereas the later one can be harvested only in the following spring. The brood bulbs can also be planted, but they will need two years before they ripen. A good, well-germinating seed source is very important for a successful planting. Don't use garlic left over from your spice shelf and don't expect much from the cloves you bring back from your vacation in the sunny south. The best approach is to buy garlic cloves in a commercial garden center or from a special seed-catalogue company.

Harvesting and Preserving:
Garlic is ripe when the leaves turn yellow and dry. Remove them carefully from the ground with the aid of a garden fork, and let the cloves dry in the sun for a day or two before you brush the dirt away and tie them together in braids. These bulbs keep well all winter long if they are hung in a cool, dry place. You can also preserve the cloves in oil or vinegar.

Onion
(Allium cepa)

Origin: Onions are probably native to the steppes of central Asia, but they have been known and loved for thousands of years in Asia, the Orient, and the regions around the Mediterranean Sea.

Botanical Description: Onions are another member of the *Liliacea* family. They can be round, elongated, or flat, with a dry outer skin that is either brownish, red, or white. A tall stem rises from between the narrow, tubelike leaves and produces at its top a spherical blossom consisting of many greenish-white individual flowers.

Cultivation: Like the garlic plant,

Garlic

the onion is not an herb, but since it has always ranked among the medicinal and spice plants of the earth, it cannot be left out of our garden. You will surely find the variety appropriate for your purposes among the many that are commercially available.

In March you can start to plant the seed bulbs in rows about 8" apart. Scallions and shallots can be planted in April, again keeping a distance of about 6" to 8" between plants. When pressing them into the soil, be sure to leave the uppermost tip of the bulb exposed to the light and air. The white spring onions should not be planted before August so that they can be harvested in the following spring.

All onions need a loose soil rich in humus and a lot of direct sun. They do not tolerate wetness or nitrogen at all. Be careful when raking, because onions have very shallow and flat roots. The hardy winter hedge onions are particularly well suited for an herb garden, because, instead of producing bulbs, they form profuse, green, scallionlike leaves.

Harvesting and Preserving:
Seed onions, scallions, and shallots ripen in late summer when their foliage turns yellow and falls over. Dig the bulbs out with a garden fork and let them dry in the sun, after which they can be cleaned, tied up in braids, or spread out on top of wooden crates. Onions are best stored in a dry but cool room. Spring onions should be eaten fresh, and pearl onions can be preserved in vinegar

Winter hedge onions produce spicy stalks.

Biennial Herbs

Caraway
(Carum carvi)

Origin: Caraway is as indigenous to all of Europe as it is to Turkey, Persia, and North Africa. It grows wild in wet fields and is one of the oldest known spices.

Botanical Description: Caraway is a member of the *Umbellifera* family. In the first year, it sets a low rosette of leaves from a long taproot. In the second year, long, grooved stalks that eventually branch out grow out of this rosette. The leaves are delicately pinnate, and white and pink umbeled blossoms appear on the tips of the stems from May to June. When ripe, the fruits fall and break apart into 2 sickle-shaped seeds.

Cultivation: Like most other biennial spices, you can sow caraway in the springtime (April) or in summer (July and August). In keeping with its native habitat, this herb likes a damp but loose soil, and it always welcomes a little lime. Since caraway seeds need light to germinate, they should lie close to the surface of the soil. The rows need about 12" to 13" between them. This spice plant grows without difficulty. It can attain a height of 4'.

Harvesting and Preserving: During the course of the summer, when the seeds turn brown, you can cut the stems off, tie them together in bunches, and hang them up to dry. You may want to set a portion of the seeds aside

for replanting next year. The rest of the harvest can be kept in a closed container and be used as a spice or as a digestive tea.

Caraway leaves in the first year (above); blossoms and seeds in the second year (below).

Biennial Herbs

Parsley
(Petroselinum crispum)

Origin: Parsley is indigenous to the southeastern regions of the Mediterranean Sea. This herb had been known and used since ancient times. Today parsley is the most popular of all kitchen spices.

Botanical Description: Parsley, too, is a member of the *Umbellifera* family. It sets a long, fleshy root into the ground and in the first year forms bushy leaves that are either pinnate or "curly." In the second year this plant develops a long, squarrose stem that bears greenish-yellow umbeled blossoms from June to July. The seeds of the parsley plant are poisonous.

Cultivation: The leafy parsley plant loves a well-drained, nutrient-containing humus soil. Choose a damp, partially shady spot and prepare the earth with compost and a handful of organic fertilizer well before you plant. Manure or other fresh animal waste is absolutely not recommended.

You can start planting this herb in open beds as early as March, and you may want to reseed again between August and September to ensure another generation of green harvests. The rows need about 4″ to 6″ distance between them, and the plant usually grows to a height of 7½″ to 12″ tall.

Parsley takes a very long time to germinate. Because of this, it is a good idea to plant a few radish seeds in the parsley rows, for these grow rapidly and thus mark the location. This will also enable you to weed the area without accidentally pulling up the pars-

Curly-leafed parsley.

Smooth-leafed parsley.

ley seeds. Remember to keep the parsley plants watered in warm weather. Another thing to remember is that parsley does not get along with its own kind, so you must be careful to plant it in a different location each year. This crop wilts and withers away if it is not rotated! You can cover the green leaves with pine branches as a winter protection.

Two varieties of parsley are available in commercial garden centers: the curly-leafed and the smooth-leafed. The luxuriantly curly sort is frequently used as a decoration, whereas the simple, smooth-leafed variety has a stronger aroma and flavor. There is also a third variety known as root parsley. You can plant this herb the same way you do the other varieties of parsley; the only difference is that these young plants need about 4″ distance between the individual specimens. Only in this way can they develop strong root systems.

Harvesting and Preserving: You can pick the fresh leaves of the parsley plant all year round, but they become bitter and distasteful once the plants have started to bloom. Autumn is a good time to transplant a few into flower pots and leave them on the windowsill. It is possible to freeze parsley, but it really doesn't pay because you can always pick fresh leaves from the open garden beds.

Root parsley should be dug up toward the end of fall and resettled either in a closed hotbed or in a sandbox in the cellar. Before doing this, however, you should carefully cut off all the leaves, making sure that you do not damage the "heart." This same procedure can be applied to carrots and celery. In this way you can keep the roots over the winter and they can be retrieved whenever they are needed in the kitchen.

Scurvy Grass
(Cochlearia officinalis)

Origin: Scurvy grass is a native of the northern coasts of Europe, where it grows wild in damp, salty spots. This herb is rich in vitamins and has been used for a very long time as a remedy for certain deficiencies, including the feared scurvy. It was highly prized by seafarers.

Botanical Description: Scurvy grass is a member of the *Crucifera* family. It develops a thin,

Scurvy Grass

Biennial Herbs

long taproot with many ancillary roots. The typical, spoon-shaped leaves grow on the lower portions of the branched and grooved stalks. The upper portions of these stems are covered with oval leaves. In the second year, scurvy grass is adorned with white flowers that appear in dense clusters from May until June.

Cultivation: In the garden as well as in its natural habitat, scurvy grass is very undemanding. It needs a damp soil and thrives even in partial shade. You can sow the seeds in open beds either in the springtime (March to April) or in late summer (August to September). The rows should be about 7½″ to 8″ apart, for the individual plants can reach a height of 8″ to 12″. One thing to remember is that this succulent herb does not like to be dry in the summer. In the winter its green leaves should be protected with a loose cover of pine or spruce branches. This easily accessible cave lets you harvest your crop even in snowy weather.

Harvesting and Preserving: Only the spoon-shaped leaves should be picked fresh and used immediately. Preserving is not necessary, since this herb remains green all year round.

Bitter Winter Cress
(*Barbarea vulgaris*)

Origin: Winter cress is indigenous to continental Europe, where it grows wild in damp ditches and along streams.

Botanical Description: Winter cress is another member of the *Crucifera* family. Its branched taproot produces a rosette of thick, multiple, pinnate leaves in the first year. In the second year the plants produce a stalk 12″ to 31″ high which branches out profusely. The upper leaves are denticulated and surround the stalk. This herb blooms from April to June in the form of bright yellow flower clusters.

Cultivation: Winter cress is easy to cultivate. You can sow the seeds in open beds from March to April or from August to September. The rows should be about 7½″ to 12″ apart. The ideal condi-

Bitter Winter Cress

tions include a damp, somewhat loamy soil and a partially shady location. You can improve the condition of light soils by adding some clay meal. These herbs must be watered during dry spells, and it is a good idea to cover the ground around the winter cress with a layer of mulch to keep the humus moist.

Harvesting and Preserving: The large leaves of the rosette can be picked fresh any time of the year. It is not worth the trouble to preserve them.

Johnny-jump-up
(Viola tricolor)

Origin: Pansies are indigenous to Europe, northern Asia, North Africa, and North America, where they grow wild in fields and meadows.

Botanical Description: Pansies and the smaller Johnny-jump-ups belong to the family of *Violaceae*. Out of a slender root grow hollow, multibranched stems with partly elongated, partly heart-shaped leaves. In addition, there are also pinnate ancillary leaves. The typical pansy blossoms with their friendly "faces" are yellowish-white, bluish-white, or blue-violet. They bloom from May to August.

Cultivation: These charming wild flowers add cheerful spots of color to the herb garden. Optimally, they live for 2 years, sometimes only 1. The small blossoms love the sun, but are otherwise

very undemanding. Almost any type of soil is agreeable to them just as long as it is not too dry. You will come across these plants only along the unsprayed edges of fields or in wild meadows. You can dig them up in the spring and transplant them to your herb bed with about 4″ to 6″ between individuals. It is also possible to gather seeds from wild Johnny-jump-ups in the late summer. These plants seed themselves easily once they have become accustomed to the garden. The larger-blossomed pansies have no medicinal properties.

Harvesting and Preserving: The entire blooming plant can be picked and dried during the summer months.

Johnny-jump-up

Biennial Herbs

Mullein
(Verbascum densiflorum)

Origin: This wild flower is native to Europe as well as to Asia Minor. It was as highly prized by the ancient Romans as a medicinal plant as it was by medical practitoners in medieval Germany.

Botanical Description: Mullein belongs to the family of the *Scrophulariaceae*. This plant forms a low rosette of large, hairy, silver-gray leaves in the first year and produces a strong, tall, fuzzy stalk in the second. The upper leaves are somewhat smaller but just as vigorous. The stalk develops candelabrum-like branches, and the stems in the upper regions are densely covered with yellow, saucer-shaped flowers from July to September.

Cultivation: In its natural habitat, mullein loves bleak, stony locations and full sun. You should try to reconstruct these conditions in your garden, perhaps by mixing some sand and stones in with the soil. As these plants reseed themselves, they sometimes choose the narrow strip between flagstones. It is a good idea to leave them there, if at all possible.

You can sow mullein seeds in a small seedbed in June or July, taking care that you keep them uniformly moist, especially during the hot weeks of summer. The small plants should be transplanted to their permanent location in the fall. Keep about 12″ to 15″ between individual specimens, because by the following year they will be at least 5′ to 6½′ tall. A little algal limestone is always welcome.

Harvesting and Preserving: Newly opened blossoms can be collected repeatedly throughout the summer. They should be picked without the calyx and very carefully spread out to dry. They must never be damp! You can also toss a few fresh blossoms into a hearty soup.

Mullein

Garden Angelica
(Angelica archangelica)

Origin: Garden angelica is indigenous to northern Europe, where it grows wild as far north as Greenland and Siberia.

Botanical Description: Angelica belongs to the *Umbellifera* family. Its fleshy roots reach deep into the ground, while its strong, tall stems are ribbed and its mighty leaves are unevenly pinnate. One distinctive characteristic of angelica is the fact that the stems of the leaves form convex pockets at the point where they are joined to the main stalk. This sizable bush blooms from July to August and its greenish-white blossom clusters smell like honey.

Cultivation: A plant as elegant as angelica, which can easily attain a height of 8′, needs a nourishing location. Plant this herb in a humus soil that has been tended with compost and an organic fertilizer. Angelica likes moisture and partial shade, but it does not tolerate standing water. If you have enough room for several plants, you must keep at least 3′ between them

Although it is possible to sow in early autumn, this is usually not worth the effort. You can buy seedlings or larger specimens in many garden centers as well as from firms specializing in herb plants. Angelica lives about 2 to 3 years, and then it dies.

Harvesting and Preserving: Tender, young leaves and their stems should be picked fresh and

Garden Angelica

used immediately. The medicinal roots should be dug up in the springtime or in the fall and dried according to the recipe on p. 53.

Fennel
(Foeniculum vulgare)

Origin: The native natural habitat of fennel is found in the lands around the Mediterranean and in Asia Minor. It is one of the ancient hard-seed spices that were used by the early Egyptians, the Greeks, and the ancient Romans.

Botanical Description: Fennel, too, is a member of the *Umbellifera* family. Its long taproot grows deep into the ground. Very delicately pinnate leaves grow on the tall, grooved, and branched stalks. It bears a strong resemblance to dill, and develops large clusters of numerous single yellow flowers from July to September. The fennel seeds look like small half-moons.

Cultivation: Tea and spice fennel grows into mighty bushes that can reach 6' or more. It needs a damp, nutrient-containing soil that ideally also contains some lime. This herb will always turn its "head" toward the sun so that the seeds ripen fully. Prepare a place for fennel in your herb garden with a generous amount of compost and some organic fertilizer. You might also want to spread a bit of algal limestone or dolomitic limestone and powdered clay in with it. The soil must be very loose and porous so that the roots can penetrate deeply.

You can buy tea-fennel plants wherever such herbs are sold. Shrub gardens also provide an attractive variety with bronze-colored foliage. Nevertheless, it is also possible to sow the seeds in a separate open bed in April or May. The rows should be 7½" to 9½" apart. These plants will need a protective cover of pine branches during the winter, and in the following spring they will be ready to be transplanted to their permanent location with about 15" to 20" between them.

Harvesting and Preserving: The seeds begin to ripen gradually toward the end of summer. Cut the brown, umbrellalike flower clusters away regularly. They can be tied together and hung up to dry. You can also pick the tender fennel leaves for use as a spice.

Fennel

Lovage
(Levisticum officinale)

Origin: Lovage is probably indigenous to southern Europe. Monks brought this herb with them across the Alps and it has been growing there ever since the days of medieval cloister gardens.

Botanical Description: Lovage is another member of the *Umbellifera* family. Strong, hollow stalks that develop branches on their upper portions grow out of a branched and deeply set root. The hearty leaves are subdivided into rhombic, pinnate leaves. Large clusters of small greenish-yellow

Lovage

blossoms appear from July to August.

Cultivation: This robust soup herb has no trouble in reaching a height of 6½′ to 10′. In order to do this, however, it needs a deep, nutrient-containing soil and adequate moisture. Give your lovage healthy doses of compost as well as some organic fertilizer. It can also use a dose of stinging-nettle liquid manure in the summer. This herb grows in the sun and in partial shade. One plant is usually sufficient for the needs of one family. If you have several bushes, you should keep them at least 20″ apart.

You can obtain lovage plants from any commercial garden center, but you can also sow them yourself in April or August. Once they have gotten accustomed to

their location, these robust plants will thrive for years without any difficulties.

Harvesting and Preserving: You can pick the tender, young leaves for use as a spice at any time, but if you intend to dry them, you should do so before the blooming season.

Winter Savory
(Satureia montana)

Origin: Winter savory is indigenous to the Mediterranean regions.

Botanical Description: Winter savory is a perennial herb belonging to the *Labiata* family. The multibranched, small shrub grows from an equally branched rhizome. Narrow, dark green leaves run along the hollow branches, the tips of which are covered in the summer with dainty whitish, pink, or violet blossoms.

Cultivation: Once spring is really here, you can place these plants in a sunny location well protected against cold winds. Winter savory thrives best in loose, sandy soil containing a little lime. It grows to a height of 7½″ to 15″ and should be surrounded by about 1 square foot of free space. If this herb receives too much nourishment, it becomes very sensitive to frost. You should protect these shrubs in rugged locations by covering them with spruce or pine branches during the winter. Propagation is possible by simply dividing the rootstocks. These

Perennial Herbs

Winter Savory

southern Europe. It was already popular in ancient times and was brought across the Alps very early on by monks.

Botanical Description: Lavender is a member of the *Labiata* family. It sinks a taproot deep into the earth. The above-ground portion forms small, multibranched semi-shrubs. The narrow greenish-gray leaves and the fragrant blue blossom spikes that appear from July to September are very characteristic of lavender.

Cultivation: Lavender flouishes willingly if you give it a sunny, dry spot with good drainage. A little lime is also good for it. Plant this herb in the garden in May about 12″ apart. You can purchase

Lavender

plants can be purchased in garden centers specializing in shrubs and bushes.

Harvesting and Preserving: Young twigs or leaves can be picked at any time, as soon as the plants are big enough. The herb should be cut just prior to the bloom if you want to dry it, but make sure that the small shrubs are left with enough strength to produce another crop.

Lavender
(Lavandula angustifolia)

Origin: Lavender is native to the Mediterranean regions of

forced lavender plants in any good shrub center, or else you can grow it yourself on the windowsill or in a greenhouse. Cut off a few branches from older lavender bushes and plant them in small pots. They should be cut back slightly after the bloom. This herb needs a protective covering of pine branches only during very harsh winters.

Harvesting and Preserving: You can pick young leaves for use as a spice at any time. If you want to dry them, you should cut off the blossoms just after they open.

Lemon Balm

Lemon Balm
(Melissa officinalis)

Origin: Lemon balm is indigenous to the Far East, but it has been naturalized for thousands of years in the regions surrounding the Mediterranean Sea. In the Middle Ages it had already made its appearance in the cloister gardens of what is now Germany.

Botanical Description: Lemon balm is a member of the *Labiata* family. It forms a branched rootstock with runners. Oval, denticulated leaves grow on squarrose, multibranched stalks. Small white or mauve blossoms appear in the leaf axils from July to August. These bushy shrubs can attain a height of 20″ to 40″.

Cultivation: Lemon balm flourishes best in humous, porous soil. It needs full sun and should be given generous amounts of compost regularly, because it can stay in the same location for many years. You can purchase lemon-balm plants in many nurseries, garden centers, and specialized garden shops in the springtime, but you can also sow it yourself in May or even force it indoors starting as early as March. Place the shrubs in the herb garden with about 12″ between plants. You can easily increase your reserve later on by dividing the large rootstocks. This herb frequently reseeds itself as well.

Harvesting and Preserving: You can pick the fresh leaves that smell like lemons at any time between spring and fall. Cut off the upper branches shortly before the bloom if you want to dry this herb.

Perennial Herbs

Bee Balm
(Monarda didyma)

Origin: Bee balm is indigenous to North America. It first came to Europe after the discovery of the New World.

Botanical Description: Bee balm, is a member of the *Labiata* family. It forms a flat-growing, many-branched rootstock. Pointed, oval, toothed leaves grow from squarrose stalks. Bee balm blooms from June to October, and its iridescent red blossoms form a slightly scrubby-looking whorl.

Cultivation: Bee balm is very undemanding; it is true that these plants thrive best in moist soil in a sunny location, but they can also flourish in dry places with partial shade. Plant the shrubs, which can grow as tall as 32″ to 60″, approximately 12″ to 15″ apart.

Bee Balm

Bee balm propagates via stolons or root runners that you can later separate from the parent and transplant. With its iridescent red blossoms and fragrant leaves, this plant will be one of the main attractions in your herb garden.

The genuine natural form of bee balm can be obtained only in very well-stocked garden centers featuring shrubs or in special retail centers dealing in herbs. The various and many-colored cultivars of bee balm are of no value for an herb garden.

Harvesting and Preserving: Fresh, tender leaves can be picked when needed. If you want to dry the leaves of this herb, be sure to pick a supply of them before the blooming season begins.

Wild Marjoram
(Origanum vulgare)

Origin: Wild marjoram is indigenous to southern Europe and Asia and has been grown in herb gardens ever since the Middle Ages.

Botanical Description: Wild marjoram is a member of the *Labiata* family. Squarrose reddish-brown stalks grow out of a flat and multi-branched rootstock. The small, oval leaves are covered with delicate hairs. From June to September the tips of the branches bloom with profuse pseudospikes of pink or white blossoms.

Cultivation: This spice plant from the south needs a very warm,

Wild Marjoram

sunny location and light, porous soil. It grows about 12″ to 20″ tall. You can purchase these plants in good nurseries and sometimes even in garden centers. They are easily propagated by carefully removing the root runners. You can also sow this herb yourself and force it on a warm windowsill. Early May is the time to plant it in the garden with about 7½″ to 10″ between the individual plants. Older wild-marjoram bushes should be cut back in the spring by removing all the dried branches and shoots very close to the ground. In very cold regions this herb needs some winter protection.

Harvesting and Preserving: Young leaves and shoots can be harvested at any time, and the plants are especially spicy during the blooming season. This is when you should frequently cut bunches to be hung up and dried.

Peppermint
(Mentha piperita)

Origin: Peppermint probably came originally from the area around the Mediterranean Sea and in western Asia. Nevertheless, it has also grown wild in western Europe for a very long time.

Botanical Description: Peppermint is yet another member of the *Labiata* family. It grows from flat roots that send out expansive runners. Elongated, oval leaves with toothed edges decorate the squarrose stems. Pseudospikes with lilac or pink blossoms bloom on the tips of the branches from July to August.

Cultivation: All mint plants love moist, humous soil and light, partial shade. Even so, they also thrive in drier and sunny locations. Since this herb grows very vigorously, you should give it a special place where it can serve as a ground cover and spread out undisturbed. If this is undesirable, you will have to restrict it by planting it in a bottomless pail or bucket.

Commercial establishments offer different varieties of mint for sale. "Genuine Mitcham Mint," which is particularly aromatic, can be propagated only via root runners. Plant these stolons in moist soil rich in compost about

Perennial Herbs

Peppermint

crop frequently ripens during the warm weeks of late summer.

Rosemary
(Rosmarinus officinalis)

Origin: Rosemary is indigenous to the Mediterranean region, where it was highly valued by all the ancient peoples.

Botanical Description: Rosemary is a member of the *Labiata* family. It grows into small, evergreen, branched bushes with narrow, needlelike leaves. Blossoms that range in color from pale blue to violet grow from the leaf axils from March to July.

Cultivation: Rosemary is not winter-hardy in much of Europe and America. Plant it in pots with a mixture of sand and humus. Once a month from April until the end of August you might want to give these plants a dose of fertilizer diluted with water. Toward the middle of May you should transplant your rosemary bushes in a very sunny, protected location in the garden. They can also stay on the balcony or on a terrace with a southern exposure. Potted plants dry out quickly, however, and you must therefore remember to water them generously when the weather is hot. During the winter the plants should be taken out of the southern exposure and brought into the house (see tips on p. 23).

8″ to 12″ apart. Be sure you carefully clear the whole area of weeds before you plant, for it will be very difficult to remove them once they have become entangled in the roots of the mint plant. Once the mint has grown into a thick and dense plant, it will shade the soil itself and thus spare you any additional work. Mint grows about 20″ to 30″ tall.

You may want to try the popular varieties with special fragrances, such as field mint, orange mint, and pineapple mint. The woolly-leafed apple mint is a very vigorously growing plant.

Harvesting and Preserving: You can pick fresh mint leaves at any time during the summer. Cut the herb shortly before the bloom if you intend to dry it. A second

Rosemary develops strong twigs, needlelike leaves, and pretty blossoms.

If you have the patience, you can grow rosemary from seed. Germination should take place on a warm windowsill or in a greenhouse (see p. 35). You can later increase the number of your rosemary plants by planting cuttings.
Harvesting and Preserving: You can always harvest a few leaves and twigs when you need them, but it is also very possible to dry entire stalks. Since rosemary is considered an ornamental plant and since it takes such a long time to grow into a small bush, most herb gardeners handle it very carefully and protectively. They frequently recommend cutting it in places where it can easily grow back and where the removal of a bit of the plant will not mar its overall appearance.

Garden Sage
(Salvia officinalis)

Origin: Garden sage is indigenous to the Mediterranean regions. Even the Greeks and Romans used it, and it was highly prized in medieval cloister gardens.
Botanical Description: Garden sage is a member of the *Labiata* family. This small, woody undershrub has a branched rootstock and squarrose stalks with grayish-green, somewhat downy leaves. The elongated shape sometimes takes the form of 2 points at its end. Sage remains green in winter and blooms with bright bluish-violet blossoms from June to August.
Cultivation: The sage bush

Perennial Herbs

Garden Sage

needs a very sunny location and loose, rather dry soil. You should add a little algal lime in addition to compost. A loamy soil must be loosened up with sand at all costs.

You can sow garden sage in a hotbed starting in April and in the open garden in May, and you can propagate it by means of cuttings or sinker shoots. Young plants should be between 12″ and 15″ apart in the herb bed. Forced or fully developed bushes can be purchased in nurseries, garden centers, or firms specializing in herbs. There are charming varieties of this medicinal and spice herb: In well-stocked garden centers you can purchase those with colored leaves as well as the coarse-leafed muscatel sage. Ornamental sage is not recommended for a spice garden.

Harvesting and Preserving:
Fresh leaves can be picked whenever they are needed. Cut off the tips of the shoots shortly before they bloom if you want to dry sage, but remember that the bush needs time to put out new shoots before the onset of winter. If it does not do this, it can easily freeze.

Common Thyme
(Thymus vulgaris)

Origin: Thyme is equally at home in the southern European Mediterranean regions and in North and West Africa. The ancient Egyptians, Romans, and Greeks prized this herb highly, and monks carried it over the Alps, where it soon became naturalized in medieval cloister gardens.

Botanical Description: Thyme is a member of the *Labiata* family. A small, branched shrub with narrow, sturdy leaves grows out of a vigorous, woody taproot. Older specimens of this evergreen herb turn woody from the inside. The small shrubs are covered from May to September with pinkish-purple blossoms that grow together in false whorls.

Cultivation: Dry, porous soil and direct sunlight are important for good growth. Thyme needs no additional nourishment besides compost; if you restrict its diet, it remains healthy. Young plants can be purchased in nurseries, garden centers, and in special establishments dealing with herbs. Each individual plant

Perennial Herbs

should have about 8 square inches to call its own. You can take cuttings from older thyme bushes in the summer or else you can grow this herb from seeds, which are best sown on a warm windowsill or in a greenhouse.

If you decide to purchase thyme plants, you will have a choice between two varieties. French or summer thyme grows low and spreads out quickly, but it is sensitive to the cold. German or winter thyme grows slowly, but is more resistant. You may also want to try lemon thyme with its refreshing fragrance. Mother-of-thyme *(Thymus serpyllum),* a field plant that also grows wild has also earned a place in the herb garden. It is cultivated the same way garden thyme is.

All varieties of thyme in rugged locations need some sort of winter protection. Carefully cut back the small shrubs in the spring so that they can set fresh new shoots.

Hyssop
(Hyssopus officinalis)

Origin: Hyssop is native to southern Europe and the Far East. Monks brought this herb with them across the Alps, and it subsequently became a highly prized specimen in medieval cloister gardens.
Botanical Description: Hyssop is

Common Thyme

a member of the *Labiata* family. Low undershrubs with woody, squarrose stems grow from a branched rootstock. The dark green leaves are very narrow. Many blossoms, which can range in color from blue to pink or white, appear in the leaf axils from July to September. Altogether they form very attractive panicles on a stem and add color to your herb garden.
Cultivation: Like most southern herbs, hyssop loves loose, somewhat dry soil and direct sun. You can feed it with a little algal lime and a few handfuls of compost. As for the rest, these shrubs, which grow about 12″ to 20″ tall, are very undemanding. You can buy young plants in many nurseries, frequently categorized under the ornamental shrubs. You can also sow this herb yourself on a

warm windowsill or in a green-house (see pp. 32–34). Young plants should be about 10" to 12" apart in an open bed. Propagation by means of cuttings is another possibility, and only in very rugged locations does hyssop need winter protection. The shrubs have to be cut back in the spring.

Hyssop

Harvesting and Preserving: Fresh leaves and sprigs can be picked continuously, but should be cut shortly before the blooming season if you want to dry them.

Elecampane
(Inula helenium)

Origin: Elecampane is probably indigenous to central Asia, but it has been naturalized in southern Europe for a very long time. It was already in use in central Europe during the Middle Ages.

Botanical Description: Elecampane is a member of the *Composita* family. Strong stems that can attain a height of 5' to 8' grow out of a deep and vigorous rootstock. The characteristics of this herb include its large, elliptical leaves that are grayish-green in color and covered with woolly hairs. The yellow blossoms of elecampane bloom from June to September.

Cultivation: You can purchase elecampane plants in good nurseries that also stock shrubs. Plant them in the open bed in the spring or fall in moist, loamy soil. These plants thrive in the sun as well as in light shade. Since they grow very tall and wide, you should keep about 20" between them. These glorious shrubs can also be used as ornamentals. They can be propagated by dividing the roots of young plants.

Harvesting and Preserving: You can dig up parts of the rootstock of older plants in the fall and leave them out to dry (see p. 53).

Costmary
(Chrysanthemum balsamita)

Origin: Costmary comes from the Orient and is one of the oldest plants in our farmers' gardens.

Botanical Description: Costmary, too, is a member of the *Composita* family. The rootstock is multibranched and produces runners. The leaves are elongated and oval and have teeth along their edges. They have an aro-

Elecampane

Harvesting and Preserving:
Tender green leaves can be harvested fresh from spring to fall. Cut the leaves prior to the bloom if you intend to dry them.

Mugwort
(*Artemisia vulgaris*)

Origin: Mugwort is at home throughout Europe, where it grows wild along the sides of paths and on rocky slopes. It is also widespread in Asia and North America.

Botanical Description: Mugwort is a member of the *Composita* family. The branched roots give rise to a vigorous, multibranched, bushy plant. The variously pinnate leaves are green on the upper side and grayish-white on the underside. The small yellow blossoms appear on long panicles in August.

matic fragrance and a pale green color. In late summer the small yellow blossoms appear on long stems.

Cultivation: You can purchase young costmary plants in well-stocked nurseries that also offer shrubs. Later on you can propagate this herb very easily by separating the root runners from the parent plant. Place these in a very sunny location with a porous but very dry soil. If need be, you can add some sand to the soil. These plants spread out in all directions because of their runners, so you should leave about 16″ to 20″ between them. These blooming shrubs can grow as tall as 24″ to 30″, but the leaves grow only half as tall.

Costmary

Cultivation: This shrub is still very widespread as an undemanding weed. It can frequently be found at construction sites, which is fortunate because no one will mind if you take a few specimens home with you. You can also purchase mugwort plants in special herb nurseries. Plant them in a very sunny location with as poor a soil as possible; a little lime is also good for them. Mugwort is otherwise completely undemanding and grows about 3′ to 5′ tall.

Harvesting and Preserving: As long as the flower buds have not yet opened, you can cut the upper branches off and hang them up to dry. The leaves should be removed later and kept or used as a tea. The dried blossoms can be used as a kitchen spice.

Southernwood
(Artemisia abrotanum)

Origin: Southernwood is indigenous to southern Europe and the Far East. Monks carried it over the Alps in the 9th or 10th century.

Botanical Description: Southernwood belongs to the *Composita* family. Tarragon, common wormwood, and mugwort are the closest relatives of this herb. It produces a multibranched, small shrub with delicately pinnate leaves all from one branched rootstock. Pale yellow, globular blossoms appear on the ends of the twigs from July to October.

Cultivation: Plant your southernwood in the springtime in a sunny location with loose soil. A little lime will never hurt, but too much nourishment and water damage these plants. Arrange to surround the small shrubs, which grow a little taller than 3′, with about 15 square inches of space. You can propagate this herb yourself by taking cuttings, but the initial plants should be purchased in a well-stocked nursery specializing in either shrubs or herbs. Southernwood needs a protective covering in cold winters. It is certainly worth the effort, though, to introduce this herb back into

Mugwort

Perennial Herbs

the garden—the aromatic plant that was so beloved in the Middle Ages but has recently fallen into relative oblivion.

Harvesting and Preserving: You can pick fresh twigs from spring until fall, but be sure you cut them before the bloom if you want to dry them. You should also take care how you cut the shrubs, for they are indeed an ornament in your herb garden.

Tarragon
(Artemisia dracunculus)

Origin: Tarragon is indigenous to southern and central Asia, Mongolia, Siberia, and North America. The Crusaders introduced it to the Mediterranean regions, and from there it made its way across the Alps.

Botanical Description: Tarragon is a member of the *Composita* family. These plants form

Southernwood

branched roots with wide-spreading runners. Narrow, elongated leaves grow on the branched stalks, and the greenish-yellow blossoms start appearing in July.

Cultivation: Herb gardeners have their choice between two varieties of tarragon, Russian and French. Russian tarragon can be sown from seed. It is a resistant variety, but not particularly aromatic. French (sometimes also called German) tarragon can be propagated only by means of root runners. It is somewhat more sensitive, but it does have an incomparably spicy aroma.

Tarragon loves a moist soil rich in humus. It thrives in sun as well as in partial shade. Give it a lot of compost, some powdered clay, and a little organic fertilizer. Russian tarragon should be sown in the open garden in April and later transplanted with about 15 square inches of space around each individual. You can plant the runners of French tarragon in the spring or the fall in a space approximately 12″ × 15″. This herb grows about 2′ to 6′ tall. You can continue to propagate this plant later on by taking root runners or cuttings and planting them yourself. Tarragon must be kept thoroughly watered during the hot weeks of summer, and it needs a pine-branch protection in harsh winters.

Harvesting and Preserving: You can harvest fresh twigs and leaves from early spring until the first frost. They should be cut before the bloom, however, if you

Perennial Herbs

Tarragon

Cultivation: You are best advised to dig up a tansy plant growing by the roadside, but they can also be purchased in nurseries specializing in herbs. This plant is very undemanding. It thrives best in dry, porous soil in direct sunshine. Tansy takes care of its own propagation by means of the many root runners it produces. No particular care is necessary. These shrubs can grow as tall as 20″ to 60″, and the ornamental leaves and iridescent blossoms add a touch of color to your herb garden.

Harvesting and Preserving: You can cut and dry the entire blooming plant during the summer months.

want to dry them, but remember that tarragon loses a part of its spicy qualities when dried. One recommendation is to preserve this herb in vinegar (see recipe on p. 57).

Common Tansy

Common Tansy
(Tanacetum vulgare)

Origin: Common tansy is indigenous to Europe and northern Asia, where it grows wild on sunny roadsides and in wasteland.

Botanical Description: Tansy is a member of the *Composita* family. Tall stalks with double pinnate leaves grow out of a multi-branched rootstock that produces many runners. This herb is adorned from June to September with loose corymbs of solidly clustered yellow blossoms.

Yarrow
(Achillea millefolium)

Origin: Yarrow, or milfoil as it is also called, in indigenous to all of Europe. Even today it grows wild in fields and along roadsides.

Botanical Description: Yarrow is another member of the *Composita* family. It continuously forms new shoots from its creeping rootstock. The first appearance in spring is a rosette with curly leaves, and out of this grow tall, stiff stalks with narrow, pinnate leaves. Flowers in the form of flat false corymbs appear on the tips of the shoots from June until autumn. These blossoms range in color from white to pink.

Cultivation: Yarrow should be planted in a sunny location about 12″ to 15″ apart. It is a very undemanding plant and grows in every kind of soil. The only thing it cannot tolerate is standing water. Yarrow grows about 15″ to 20″ tall. You can propagate this bush yourself by dividing the roots, and the best way to find your first plants is by taking a walk in open nature. Yarrow frequently grows in fields or along unsprayed roadsides. If this is not possible, you can order this medicinal herb from appropriate nurseries or garden centers. The yellow and red ornamental varieties of yarrow are absolutely worthless in an herb garden.

Harvesting and Preserving: The tender leaves on the early spring shoots should be picked fresh for salads. The entire blooming plant

Yarrow

can be cut and dried from June until September.

Common Wormwood
(Artemisia absinthium)

Origin: Common wormwood is indigenous to Europe and Asia. It grows in stony, dry soils.

Botanical Description: Common wormwood is also a member of the *Composita* family. A multi-branched, small shrub with silvery-gray pinnate leaves grows out of a strong rootstock. Loose panicles of round yellow blossoms appear from July to September.

Cultivation: In its native habitat or in an herb garden, wormwood thrives best in poor soil with direct sun. If need be, you can mix some sand and stones into the soil. A bit of lime is also good for this herb.

In case you need several shrubs, you should make sure you plant them 15″ to 20″ apart. Propagation is possible by means of cuttings, division, or seedings. Already flourishing plants can be purchased in many nurseries or garden centers. Wormwood grows between 2′ and 6′ tall and develops into elegant, ornamental bushes that need hardly any care. Well-stocked shrub nurseries also offer smaller varieties of wormwood, but these do not have any medicinal properties.

Harvesting and Preserving: Individual leaves can be picked fresh at any time for use as a spice. This herb should be cut before the bloom if you intend to dry it, and,

according to old recipes, wormwood can also be preserved in wine.

Horseradish
(Armoracia lapathifolia)

Origin: The horseradish plant is indigenous to southeastern Europe, but it has been growing in German gardens ever since the 12th century.

Botanical Description: Horseradish is a member of the *Crucifera* family. It forms long, strong roots, and the slender lateral roots can be removed and used to propagate new plants. These lateral roots are called vines. The firm, long leaves of this herb are curved on the edges. A cluster of white blossoms blooms atop a tall stem.

Cultivation: Horseradish is a robust herb that needs a lot of room. Once it has taken hold in its location, it is very difficult to remove it, for this plant sets new shoots out of the tiniest pieces of rootstock. This plant is not recommended for small herb gardens. You would do better to plant it in a corner of the garden near the compost heap or near a hedge.

Horseradishes love moist, nutritious humus. Compost, organic fertilizers, and a mulch layer ensure good growth. You can obtain vines from well-stocked seed-distributors, from many mail-order establishments, and, with a bit of luck, from a garden

Common Wormwood

or even your neighbor. Place the rootstocks on an angle in the soil about 12″ to 15″ apart, starting about March. 2 or 3 horseradish plants are more than enough for the needs of one family; the shrubs grow about 3′ tall and are very bushy.

Harvesting and Preserving: As soon as the plants are large enough, you can cut off fresh pieces of root whenever you need them. You should also dig up a few larger roots for your winter supply; they can be kept in the cellar or in damp sand in a hotbed.

Horseradish vines for planting.

Stinging Nettle
(Urtica dioica and Urtica urens)

Origin: Stinging nettles are native to Europe and widely distributed elsewhere. They grow in wasteland and in the vicinity of houses and gardens.

Botanical Description: Stinging nettles belong to the family of the *Urticaceae;* they form a multi-branched rootstock with long runners. The upright, squarrose stalks, like the elongated, heart-shaped leaves, are covered with stinging hairs that contain the nettle toxin. Panicles of small greenish blossoms appear in the leaf axils from May to July. The large and small varieties are distinguished solely by their size; their ingredients are almost the same.

Cultivation: Most gardeners consider stinging nettles a nuisance weed. Their good qualities as a medicinal plant and as a cost-free fertilizer-producer for organic gardens make these plants so valuable that they deserve a place in our book.

Do not plant your stinging nettles in the herb garden, because they will soon take it over. A carefully controlled number of plants,

The harvest of large horseradish roots.

however, may grow near the compost heap, beneath fruit trees, or in a hidden corner near the fence. Nettles love a soil rich in humus and nitrogen. Only recently has it become possible to purchase seeds for these plants. You need resort to this, however, only if your garden has undergone radical procedures of eliminating every single weed.

Harvesting and Preserving: The tender spring shoots can be used as fresh spices or vegetables. If you want to dry this herb, you must cut it before it sets its seeds —that is, between May and August. If you harvest early, you can expect several additional crops during one season.

Stinging Nettle

Stonecrop
(Sedum acre)

Origin: Stonecrop is indigenous to central Europe. It grows wild in sunny locations with sandy soils.
Botanical Description: Stonecrop is a member of the *Crassulacea* family. Its roots grow flat and lawnlike. The shoots with their succulent, pointed leaves are green or bluish-green. Corymbs of yellow, star-shaped blossoms appear on tall stalks from June to August.
Cultivation: Stonecrop thrives best in poor, porous soils in direct sunlight. A rock garden or a dry southern exposure is a good location for this plant. You can purchase plants in shrub nurseries as well as in special herb outlets. Plant them flat in the ground about 4″ to 6″ apart. In time, stonecrop will form a dense ground cover. Propagation is simple: Every piece of this plant that breaks off can be replanted in the soil. It will soon set its own roots.
Harvesting and Preserving: Fresh green twigs can be picked when needed. These plants remain green all year round.

Salad Burnet
(Sanguisorba minor)

Origin: Salad burnet is probably indigenous to the area surrounding the Mediterranean Sea. It has been growing wild along the dry

Stonecrop

edges of fields and roadsides in Europe for a very long time.

Botanical Description: Salad burnet is a member of the *Rosacea* family. It forms branched roots out of which grows a dense tuft of delicately pinnate leaves. Round reddish-green blossoms bloom on long stems from May to June.

Cultivation: Loose, humous soil that contains some lime and direct sunlight provide the ideal growing conditions for salad burnet. This herb can tolerate dryness more easily that it can too much moisture. You should sow salad burnet directly in the garden from April onward. The rows should be about 12″ apart, and you can later thin them out so that there is one plant every 8″ or so. Salad burnet usually wilts when transplanted because its roots have a difficult time taking hold. Nevertheless, you can try it if you wish. If you cut the blossoms at the right time and place them in a vase, the leaves remain tender for a longer period of time.

Harvesting and Preserving: You can pick fresh leaves as long as the supply lasts. It does not pay to preserve this herb, but the plant does remain green long into the winter if the weather is mild.

Common Rue
(Ruta graveolens)

Origin: The native habitat of the common rue is found in the southern European lands along the Mediterranean and in the Middle East. This herb was already known and used in ancient times, and Charlemagne made a point of including it in his gardens.

Botanical Description: Common rue is a member of the *Rutacea* family. A branched bush with smooth stalks grows out of a strong, woody rootstock. The pretty pinnate leaves are bluish-

Salad Burnet

green in color. Small yellow terminal blossoms appear in June and July; most of these blossoms have 4 petals, but the central blossom in a false cyme has 5 petals.

Cultivation: The location for common rue absolutely must have good drainage. This herb thrives well in loose, sandy soil and full sunlight. Once in a while you should add a little lime. You can sow this plant in the open garden in April, but you can also purchase healthy specimens in good garden centers and herb nurseries. Plant the small herbs about 12″ to 15″ apart. They will need very little care once they have taken root, and a winter protection of pine branches is required only in rugged areas. You can also take cuttings from older plants if you want to increase the number of decorative shrubs in your garden.

Common Rue

Harvesting and Preserving: You can pick individual leaves at any time. Common rue also remains green throughout most of the winter.

Pelargonium
(Pelargonium citriodorium)

Origin: Leaf pelargoniums are indigenous to South Africa. The first specimens reached Europe in 1690.

Botanical Description: Pelargonium is a member of the *Geraniacea* family. It forms an herbal bush with hairy stems and lobed or pinnate leaves that are likewise covered with hairs. Cymes of relatively insignificant blossoms in pink, lavender, or red appear on long stems throughout the whole summer.

Cultivation: Like the rosemary plant, the pelargonium plant is not winter-hardy in a temperate climate. It should be kept in large pots and spend the whole summer outside. Fill these pots or tubs with a loose mixture of ripe compost, sand, and peat. From spring until summer the pelargonium plant needs a lot of water and direct sunshine. During its growing period you should give it one or two doses of liquid manure diluted with water every month.

Bring the plants indoors before the first frost and let them spend the winter on a cool, bright windowsill. During this time they will not need very much water. If it is necessary, you should repot these plants starting in March; this is also a good time to cut them back a bit. You can keep some cuttings from the tips you have removed, for these grow very easily in sandy soil. Older pelargonium plants can grow as tall as 12" to 40".

It is frequently a difficult task to find varieties of pelargonium—the most likely sources are your neighbor's windowsill or botanical gardens.

The leaves of the pelargonium smell like fresh lemons. Rose geraniums *(Pelargonium graveolens)* give off a spicy, roselike aroma; woolly pelargonium *(Pelargonium tomentosum)* has a very intense smell like a peppermint candy and it has beautiful, velvety leaves. There are additionally the apple- and apricot-scented varieties. The search for these unique sources of unsuspected fragrances is worth all the trouble it entails, because these plants enrich every herb garden with magical fragrances.

Harvesting and Preserving: Individual leaves can be picked and used as a spice at any time of the year.

Forest Mallow
(Malva silvestris)

Origin: Forest mallow is indigenous to Europe and central Asia. It has been used as a medicinal plant since time immemorial.

Scented-leafed geraniums growing in motley confusion. White variegated leaves: rose geraniums. Large green leaves: peppermint geraniums. In between: lemon-scented geraniums.

Botanical Description: Mallows are members of the *Malvacea* family. They sink a long taproot into the ground and develop branched, hairy stems. Their leaves are lobed in the shape of a hand. Characteristic of all mallows is the fact that the pink and lilac-colored, dish-shaped flowers develop in the leaf axils.

Cultivation: You will find wild mallow growing in open landscapes in sunny but rather poor soil conditions along the edges of fields. You should try your best to approximate this habitat in your garden. This attractive, medicinal herb is undemanding in all other respects. Depending upon the

111

variety, it can range in height from 15" to 6'. Plant these herbs about 12" to 15" apart. Wild mallow can be purchased only in special herb nurseries. In addition to forest mallow, there is a whole series of pretty relatives, including, for example, musk mallow *(Malva moschata)* and hollyhock mallow *(Malva althaea)*. All contain effective medicinal properties —primarily mucin, which helps alleviate coughing.

A very beautiful addition to your herb garden is the hollyhock plant *(Althaea rosea)* with reddish-black mallow blossoms. The different varieties of mallow are either biennial or perennial.

Harvesting and Preserving: Tie the whole plant, including the blossoms, in a bunch and hang it up to dry. You can also harvest the blossoms of the hollyhock plant.

Forest Mallow

Common St.-John's-wort
(Hypericum perforatum)

Origin: St.-John's-wort is indigenous to Europe and Asia and ranks among the earliest medicinal plants.

Botanical Description: St.-John's-wort is a member of the *Hypericacea* family. It has branched roots that produce runners and a squarrose stalk with elongated and tapered leaves. The tips of the branches are covered with loose cymes of yellow blossoms from June to August.

There are several varieties of St.-John's-wort, and all are very similar at first glance. The only one that possesses any effective medicinal properties, however, is the "perforated" genuine St.-John's-wort. These are the important characteristics: The stalk is double-edged; the leaves are covered with transparent spots as if they had been pierced with a needle. If you hold them up against the light, you will see these "holes" very clearly. They are the glands that contain the essential oil and resin. If you squeeze a bud between your fingers, a blood-red sap will ooze out.

Cultivation: Genuine St.-John's-wort thrives preferably along sunny roadsides in poor, dry soil. Try to give it a similar location in your herb garden. A lot of light and good drainage are very important; in all other respects this plant is very undemanding. It propagates itself in good locations by means of root runners.

These plants need about 12″ to 16″ between them, and they can grow to a height of 2′ to 3½′. The simplest thing is to dig up a shrub growing along the roadside, for you can purchase St.-John's-wort only in special nurseries. The ornamental varieties are worthless for the herb garden.

Harvesting and Preserving: St.-John's-wort reaches its highest concentration of medicinal properties toward the end of June. Cut the entire blooming plant and hang it up to dry. Another recommendation is to preserve this herb in oil (see recipe, p. 57)

Comfrey
(Symphytum officinale and *Symphytum peregrinum)*

Origin: Comfrey is indigenous to all of Europe and to western Asia. It grows wild in moist meadows and along the banks of streams.

Botanical Description: Comfrey is a member of the *Boraginacea* family. It develops dark, succulent roots that extend very deep into the ground, and branches grow from coarse, hairy stalks that are highly water-retentive. The bell-shaped blossoms appear from May to September, and according to the variety, can range from creamy white to pink to blue or dusty violet.

Cultivation: Like borage, this highly water-retentive herb with its large leaves needs a moist, deep, and nutrient-containing soil. If the soil is poor, you might want to add generous amounts of compost and powdered clay directly into the plant pit. A mulch cover keeps the soil moist. Comfrey thrives in sun as well as in partial shade. It needs a lot of room because the plants can reach a height of 3′ to 6′ and tend to spread out sideways as well. Plant them about 15″ to 20″ apart. Comfrey can be purchased in shrub nurseries and in other specialized establishments, but you can propagate young shrubs easily by separating the roots. Old plants are anchored so deeply in the ground that they cannot be moved.

Harvesting and Preserving: Tender, young leaves can be picked fresh in the spring and summer. May is the most favorable time to collect leaves for drying. In early spring and late autumn you can dig up the roots and dry them, too.

Common St.-John's-wort

113

Perennial Herbs

Common Valerian
(Valeriana officinalis)

Origin: Common valerian is indigenous to central Europe, where it grows wild along the banks of streams and along the edges of meadows and forests. This herb is equally at home in central Asia and Asia Minor.

Botanical Description: Valerian is a member of the *Valerianacea* family. Its branched rootstock gives rise to furrowed stalks with deeply cut, pinnate leaves. It blooms from July to August in the form of small cymes of fragrant pinkish-white blossoms.

Cultivation: Valerian can be found in natural locations with moist as well as dry soils. Thus you can choose among the available locations in your herb garden. This herb thrives in full sun and in light, partial shade. It likes generous amounts of compost. You should plant the valerian specimens about 12″ to 15″ apart; the shrubs range in height from 3′ to 5′. You can obtain these plants in shrub and specialty nurseries, but if you proceed carefully, you may dig up a shrub along a meadow's edge and propagate it in your garden by dividing it.

Harvesting and Preserving: Remove a portion of the medicinal roots from older, already well-established plants in the fall. These should be dried according to the directions on p. 53. The characteristic valerian scent that is so attractive to cats develops only after the herb is dried.

Comfrey

Sweet Violet
(Viola odorata)

Origin: Sweet violets are indigenous to Europe. They grow wild beneath hedges and shrubs and beside paths as well as along the edge of forests.

Botanical Description: Sweet violets are members of the *Violacea* family. The rootstock spreads out widely in the ground and produces heart-shaped leaves. The typical violet blossoms appear from March to April. These fragrant blossoms are sometimes also white or pink.

Cultivation: Sweet violets love partially shady locations with moist, loose humus. They can be planted beneath woody plants to form a ground cover if the shadows and the pressure from the roots are not too great. These modest flowers flourish very self-confidently if they find favorable conditions. Leaf compost and a little organic fertilizer do a world of good. Plant your violets about 8″ to 10″ apart and keep the soil uniformly moist in the beginning.

You can purchase sweet-violet plants in every good nursery or garden center, but make sure that you are buying the genuine, fragrant sweet violet. The large-

Common Valerian

blossomed cultivars are not to be used as medicinal plants.

Harvesting and Preserving: The freshly opened blossoms and the young leaves can be picked and dried in the springtime (March to April). In the fall (October) you can dig up and dry the roots according to the directions on p. 53.

Garden Sorrel or Sour Dock
(Rumex acetosa)

Origin: Garden sorrel, or sour dock as it is also called, is indigenous to central Europe. It grows wild in moist meadows and along the edges of ditches.

Botanical Description: Sour dock belongs to the *Polygonacea* family. From its taproot, which branches out in the soil, grow smooth, arrow-shaped leaves. Sour dock produces tall reddish stems with pale pink blossom panicles from May until July.

Cultivation: In the garden as in the open meadow, sour dock loves a moist soil rich in humus. You can safely add generous amounts of compost and a little powdered clay. Partially shady spots are ideal, but this robust herb also grows in the sun.

Sweet Violet

Perennial Herbs

You can sow sour dock in April in rows with about 8″ to 10″ between plants. Later on you should thin them out until you have holes of about 4″ to 6″ in the rows. Despite the long taproot, these young plants tolerate transplanting very well. Propagation is possible via root division. If you extract a portion of the bloom at the right time, you will be able to harvest more leaves. Sour dock needs watering during prolonged hot weather; otherwise it makes no particular demands.

Harvesting and Preserving: Pick only the tender, young leaves. Preserving is not worth the effort.

Garden Sorrel

Chive
(Allium schoenoprasum)

Origin: Chives are indigenous to Europe, where they grow wild in moist locations.

Botanical Description: Chives are members of the *Liliacea* family and are related to onions. A dense root ball produces numerous tubelike leaves. Reddish-violet spherical blossoms bloom on long, stiff stems from June to August. The black seeds ripen well and are easily distributed.

Cultivation: The succulent chive shrubs flourish best in nutrient-containing, somewhat limy, moist humus. Give these plants generous amounts of compost and some organic fertilizer. In the early summer they can be given a dose of stinging-nettle liquid manure. Full sun and partial shade are equally good for chives.

Plant each individual specimen in about 8 square inches of space. Plants in small containers are available in nurseries and garden centers everywhere. Chives can also be sown in the open garden starting in April. When the tender blades have grown a few centimeters tall, take a bunch of young plants and place them all around. In this way chives develop rapidly into thick, round shrubs that can reach a height of 8" to 10" and can be easily divided in the spring. This is the best way to restock your chive plants.

Harvesting and Preserving: Always cut the spicy blades fresh; they taste best in the springtime. Remember to take only a portion of each shrub at a time so that the plant has a chance to recuperate. It does not pay to preserve chives. A better idea is to plant a root ball in a flower pot and let it grow on the windowsill during the winter.

Chives

Brief Guide to Herbs

Annual Herbs	Important Ingredients	Fragrance and Taste
Anise (p. 66)	essential oils (anethol), albumin, fat, sugar, resin	sweet and spicy
Camomile (p. 72)	essential oils (blue azulene), glucosides, bitter principles, flavones	typical, somewhat straw-like camomile scent
Celery (p. 69)	essential oils, trace elements, vitamins	intensely spicy, slightly sweet, typical celery fragrance
Chervil (p. 67)	essential oils, glucosides, bitter principles	sweetly spicy, a little like anise
Common Borage (p. 78)	mucin, tannic acid, saponin, silicic acid, minerals	freshly sour, a little like cucumber
Common Nasturtium (p. 75)	sulfur, vitamins	fresh, a little like cress, slightly sharp
Coriander (p. 68)	essential oils, fatty oils, albumin, tannin	seeds: spicy, sweet
Dill (p. 66)	essential oils, fatty oils	leaves: fresh, sharp spice; seeds: similar to caraway seeds
Garden Pepper Cress (p. 74)	essential mustard oil, vitamin C, bitter principles	piquant, somewhat peppery sharp
Garlic (p. 80)	essential oils, vitamins A, B, C, antibiotic substances (allicin), hormonelike substances	penetrating, typical garlic odor
Onion (p. 81)	essential mustard oil, vitamin C, glucosides	sharply spicy, biting, slightly sour, typical onion smell
Orach (p. 78)	saponin	spinachlike, slightly bitter
Pot marigold (p. 73)	essential oils, bitter principles, pigments, mucin, resin	strong, resinous fragrance
Purslane (p. 76)	vitamins	fresh, sour, slightly salty

Brief Guide to Herbs

Use as Seasoning	Medicinal Effect	Use as Home Remedy
baked goods, sauces, soups	relieves coughing and flatulence	tea with fennel and caraway
—	prevents swelling, relieves cramps, antibacterial against colds	tea, vaporizers
soups, stews, sauces	diuretic	—
soups, salads, sauces omelets	stimulates metabolism	fresh juice for spring cures
salads, cucumbers, cottage cheese, cold sauces	cardiac stimulant, invigorating, soothes rheumatic pains	tea, freshly minced leaves in milk
leaves and blossoms: salads; buds and young seeds: substitute for capers	invigorating, mild purgative	—
gingerbread, preserving spice (red beets)	relieves stomach and intestinal cramps	—
leaves: salads, sauces, herbed butter, fresh herbed vinegar; seeds and blossoms: pickles, herbed vinegar	relaxing, relieves flatulence	tea, dill seeds together with caraway and fennel
salads, eggs, sauces, cottage cheese	stimulates metabolism	spring cure with fresh herbs
meats, sauces, salads, soups, used in dishes of southern countries	antibacterial, lowers blood pressure, helps prevent the aging process, generally invigorating	garlic juice
salads, meats, soups, sauces, cottage cheese, potatoes	disinfectant, antiseptic, healing, stimulates appetite and digestion, soothes coughing	onion juice, syrup, poultices
salads, spinachlike vegetables	improves digestion	—
salads, soups, flower petals as substitute for saffron	heals wounds and inflammations	tea, oil, salve
salads, soups, sauces spinachlike vegetables	cleanses the blood	—

Annual Herbs	Important Ingredients	Fragrance and Taste
Summer Savory (p. 71)	essential oils, tannin	very spicy, a little biting, peppery
Sweet Basil (p. 70)	essential oils, tannin	fiery spicy, peppery, sweet, unique
Sweet Marjoram (p. 72)	essential oils, fatty oils, tannin, bitter principles	intensely sweet and spicy, typical marjoram scent
Winter purslane (p. 77)	vitamins	freshly sour

Biennial Herbs	Important Ingredients	Fragrance and Taste
Bitter Winter Cress (p. 86)	essential mustard oil, vitamins	strong, spicy, cresslike
Caraway (p. 83)	essential oils, resin, tannin	slightly biting, typical caraway fragrance
Johnny-jump-up (p. 87)	saponin, tannin and bitter principles	—
Mullein (p. 88)	mucin, saponin, small quantities of essential oils	slightly honeylike
Parsley (p. 84)	essential oils, vitamin C, minerals	sharp, spicy fragrance, invigorating, somewhat sharp spice
Scurvy Grass (p. 85)	essential mustard oil, vitamin C, tannin, bitter principles	slightly sharp, cresslike, a little salty

Perennial Herbs	Important Ingredients	Fragrance and Taste
Garden Angelica (p. 89)	essential oils, angelic acid, tannin, bitter principles, resin	strong, spicy fragrance, musklike; leaves smell like honey, stems like apples
Bee Balm (p. 94)	essential oils	fresh, spicy, reminiscent of lemon-like lemon balm and mint
Chive (p. 117)	essential oils, vitamin C, minerals	strong and spicy, a little sharp like onions
Comfrey (p. 113)	alkaloids, mucin, inulin, gum, resin, aspartic acid, tannin, allantoin	leaves: fresh, similar to borage

Use as Seasoning	Medicinal Effect	Use as Home Remedy
green beans, stews, potato dishes, meats	relieves cramps, improves digestion	tea
tomatoes, herb sauces, salads, chicken dishes, Italian vegetable dishes	relieves the stomach and intestinal area, calms the nerves	tea
meats, stews, sausages, chopped meats, potatoes, sauces	relieves cramps, strengthens nerves, warms the stomach, stimulates the appetite	tea, marjoram salve
salads	improves the body's natural resistance	—

Use as Seasoning	Medicinal Effect	Use as Home Remedy
salads	stimulates metabolism	—
cabbage, meat, cheese, stews, cottage cheese, bread	relieves flatulence, beneficial to the stomach	tea, together with fennel and anise
—	relieves coughing, cleanses the blood	tea
blossoms as a soup seasoning	decongestant for coughs and bronchitis	tea
salads, sauces, potatoes, vegetables, soups	diuretic, increases the body's resistance with vitamin C	—
salads	stimulates metabolism	—

Use as Seasoning	Medicinal Effect	Use as Home Remedy
young leaves and stems: soups, sauces, salads	roots: stimulates the appetite, relieves cramps to a slight extent, soothes nervous stomach	tea, start with cold water and bring to a slow boil; bath additive; angelica wine
fruit drinks, jellies, fruit salad, tea	—	—
salads, tomatoes, cottage cheese, eggs, sauces, omelets	stimulates the appetite, good for the stomach and bowels, bloodforming	—
leaves: salad, spinachlike vegetables	roots: heals wounds, soothes muscle strains and inflammations	tea made of roots, poultice, salve

Perennial Herbs	Important Ingredients	Fragrance and Taste
Common Rue (p. 109)	essential oils, flavone-glucosides, rutin, alkaloids	uniquely spicy, sharply bitter
Common Valerian (p. 114)	essential oils, alkaloids, tannin, resin	typical valerian scent
Common Wormwood (p. 105)	essential oils, bitter principles (absinthe), flavones, tannin, vitamin C and B_6	bitter, aromatic
Costmary (p. 100)	essential oils, tannin, bitter principles	leaves: scent like lemons and mint; slightly bitter taste
Elecampane (p. 100)	essential oils (elecampane camphor, azulene), inulin	sharp and bitter
Fennel (p. 89)	essential oils, fatty oils, minerals	sweetly spicy
Forest Mallow (p. 111)	mucin, tannin, malvin	—
Garden Sorrel (Sour Dock) (p. 115)	oxalic acid, potassium oxalate, tannin, vitamin C	fresh and sour
Horseradish (p. 106)	mustard-oil glucoside, sulfur, vitamin C	sharp and biting
Hyssop (p. 99)	essential oils, tannin, bitter principles	uniquely spicy, a little like mint
Lavender (p. 92)	essential oils, resin, tannin	fragrance: fresh and spicy; taste: sharply bitter, somewhat like rosemary
Lemon Balm (p. 93)	essential oils, tannin, bitter principles, mucin	fresh lemon fragrance and taste
Lovage (p. 90)	essential oils, resin, bitter principles, sugar	strongly spicy, a little like celery
Mugwort (p. 101)	essential oils (eucalyptus), bitter principles, inulin, tannin, resin	strongly spicy, somewhat bitter

Use as Seasoning	Medicinal Effect	Use as Home Remedy
small amounts in salads, sauces, with mutton and cheese	this herb is poisonous in large amounts; originally used for head and eye aches	—
—	calms the nerves, soothes agitated heart, anxiety, sleep disturbances	tea, tincture
fatty meats, stews, venison	makes heavy foods more easily digestible; good for stomach ailments	tea
salads, omelets, herbed butter	relieves stomach and menstrual discomforts	tea, bath additive, sachets against moths and insects
—	decongestant, soothes irritating coughing	tea, start with cold water and bring to a slow boil
fish, sauces, pork, soups, baked goods	relieves cramps, soothes flatulence	tea
—	decongestant for coughs and bronchitis	tea with warm water
salads, sauces, cottage cheese	blood cleansing, spring cure together with cress and stinging nettles	—
sauces, fish, lox, eggs, cottage cheese	internally: diuretic; externally: poultice against rheumatism	freshly pulverized roots
small amounts in salads and sauces, herbed vinegar	stimulates the appetite, relieves cramps	tea
unique seasoning for fish, sauces, fowl	strengthens the nerves, refreshing, relieves cramps	lavender oil, lavender spirits, sachets, moth-repellent bouquets
salads, sauces, cottage cheese, eggs, tomatoes	calms the heart and nerves, relieves cramps, promotes sleep	tea, baths, herb sachets
soups, sauces, stews	diuretic, relieves flatulence	tea made from dried roots
roasts, fatty meats	makes heavy dishes more easily digestible, stimulates the appetite, relieves cramps	tea

Perennial Herbs	Important Ingredients	Fragrance and Taste
Pelargonium (p. 110)	essential oils	depending upon the variety, these scents are reminiscent of lemons, old roses, peppermint, and apples
Peppermint (p. 95)	essential oils (menthol), tannin, bitter principles	typical, refreshing peppermint scent, taste slightly burning, then cool
Rosemary (p. 96)	essential oils (camphor), tannin, bitter principles, resin	fragrance: intense and spicy, like camphor and pine needles; taste: strongly spicy, a little bitter
Garden Sage (p. 97)	essential oils (among them camphor), tannin, bitter principles, saponin	strong and spicy aroma, somewhat harsh and camphorlike
Common St.-John's-wort (p. 112)	essential oils, flavone-glucoside, hyperin, tannin, pectin, red pigments	slightly resinous
Salad Burnet (p. 108)	tannin, flavones	fresh, slightly sour
Southernwood (p. 102)	essential oils, tannin, bitter principles, alkaloids	strong lemon scent, very aromatic
Stinging Nettle (p. 107)	nettle toxin, allergens, formic acid, vitamin C	spinachlike but strong, somewhat bitter
Stonecrop (p. 108)	mucin, tannin	delicately sour
Sweet Violet (p. 114)	saponin, essential oils, blue pigments	sweet violet fragrance
Common Tansy (p. 104)	essential oils, among them camphor, bitter principles	fragrance: sweet, strongly spicy
Tarragon (p. 103)	essential oils, tannin, bitter principles	delicately spicy, slightly sweet
Common Thyme (p. 98)	essential oils, resin, tannin, bitter principles	strong and spicy, somewhat sharp
Wild Marjoram (p. 94)	essential oils (thymol), tannin, bitter principles	thymelike, strongly aromatic
Winter Savory (p. 91)	essential oils, tannin	strongly spicy, slightly peppery
Yarrow (Milfoil) (p. 105)	essential oils (blue azulene), bitter principles, tannin, resin	delicately spicy, a little sharp

Use as Seasoning	Medicinal Effect	Use as Home Remedy
drinks, gelees, sweet desserts, sauces	—	—
sauces, marinades, lamb dishes	relieves cramps, warming, good for the stomach and bowels	tea, sachets, peppermint oil
meat, tomatoes, sauces, used in vegetable dishes of southern countries	stimulates circulation, strengthens the nerves	tea, sachets, baths
meat, sauces, ragouts, ham, eels, cheese	antiseptic, prevents inflammations, astringent; for sore throats, bleeding gums, night sweats	tea, in water for gargling
—	externally: heals burns and nerve/rheumatic pains; internally: calms nerves	tea, red St. John's oil
salads, sauces, cottage cheese, eggs	—	—
small amounts in salads and sauces	stimulates the appetite, strengthens the stomach	tea, moth-repellent bouquets
salads, soups, vegetables	stimulates the appetite, soothes rheumatic pains	tea, fresh juice
salads, sauces	—	—
blossoms for old-fashioned desserts, violet vinegar	relieves coughing	tea from blossoms, leaves, and roots
—	formerly used as an anthelmintic; today it is no longer used as an antitoxin	dried herb used against insects, flies, vermin
salads, sauces, fowl, fish	stimulates appetite, good for stomach, bowels	—
meat, stews, sauces, potato dishes	disinfectant, antiseptic, relieves cramps; good for coughing	tea, baths, sachets
meat, sauces, soups, stews, pizza, tomatoes	strengthens the nerves, relieves cramps	tea, in water for gargling
beans, stew, meats, potato dishes	relieves stomach and intestinal cramps	tea
young leaves with salads, eggs, and cottage cheese	appetite stimulant, soothes cramps and inflammations, relieves stomach, intestinal, and bowel discomforts	tea, baths

Index

Index

Look for these other books in the Macmillan Gardening series

THE MACMILLAN BOOK OF ORGANIC GARDENING
by Marie-Luise Kreuter

THE MACMILLAN BOOK OF ORNAMENTAL GARDENING
by Otto Hahn

Look for these other gardening books from Macmillan

WYMAN'S GARDENING ENCYCLOPEDIA
by Donald Wyman

THE TREASURY OF HOUSEPLANTS
by Rob Herwig and Margot Schubert

THE MACMILLAN TREASURY OF HERBS
by Ann Bonar